Chicken

Poop

for the Soul

Chicken
Poop
for the Soul

Stories to Harden the Heart and Dampen the Spirit

A parody by
David Fisher

POCKET BOOKS
New York   London   Toronto   Sydney   Tokyo   Singapore

This book is a work of fiction. Names, characters, places and incidents are products of the author's imagination or are used fictitiously. Any resemblance to actual events or locales or persons, living or dead, is entirely coincidental.

An *Original* Publication of POCKET BOOKS

POCKET BOOKS, a division of Simon & Schuster Inc.
1230 Avenue of the Americas, New York, NY 10020

Copyright © 1997 by David Fisher

All rights reserved, including the right to reproduce this book or portions thereof in any form whatsoever. For information address Pocket Books, 1230 Avenue of the Americas, New York, NY 10020

ISBN: 0-671-01442-0

First Pocket Books trade paperback printing October 1997

10 9 8 7 6 5 4 3

POCKET and colophon are registered trademarks of Simon & Schuster Inc.

Cover design by Brigid Pearson
Cover photo by Picture Perfect

Printed in the U.S.A.

This book is dedicated, with love, to my sister, Bette Langsam, my brother, Richard Langsam, and his wife, Elise Hagoue Langsam, who know the real meaning of chicken soup.

Acknowledgments

The author gratefully acknowledges the assistance of Patty Brown and John Boswell, of John Boswell Associates, because John might complain if I don't. I was very fortunate to have an editor who got the jokes, and pushed a little harder, Emily Bestler. And I am truly grateful to those people who answered their telephones and listened to these stories and laughed in most of the right places: Rosemary Rogers, Joanne Curtis, Laura Vertullo, and Laura Stevens.

I would especially like to thank the entire sales force of Pocket Books, perhaps the finest group of men and women ever to sell a book. I know these people will be as honored as I will be to sell many, many copies of this one in particular. Although I will get the money, they will get the satisfaction of a job well done, which I'm sure they understand is worth far more than a few bucks. Or a lot of bucks if they really believe that.

I specifically do not acknowledge any assistance from Ward Calhoun, of John Boswell Associates, who answered the telephone but would not listen to these stories, although he claims to have read them at a later time.

Contents

CONTENTS

Chicken
Poop
for the Soul

Dad's Lessons

SOMETIMES LATE AT NIGHT, WHEN THE HOUSE IS SO QUIET I can hear the familiar complaints of the friendly old floorboards stretching their limbs, and the house is warmed by love, I tiptoe into my four-year-old son's room and sit on the floor in a corner, and I just watch him sleep. His clothes are always strewn around the room, while his baseball cap hangs proudly on the doorknob. I always have to be careful not to trip over his "Big League Football," which I know to be lying somewhere in the dark. He sleeps so peacefully, so securely, I could sit there all night. And as I watch him, in these quiet moments, I can't help but remember my old man and the lessons he taught me about life.

While once I thought my dad was just about the biggest man in the whole wide world, in fact he was quite small, and thin, and his face was as cracked and pockmarked as the old leather seats of his beloved '52 Pontiac.

1

Dad had grown up dirt-poor on the great American plains. As a boy he had watched the once fertile farmland turn into the infamous Dustbowl. He often told me, "They called it the Dustbowl 'cause every night my momma would take me and my brother outside with our wooden bowls and fill 'em to the top with dust. 'That's it, boys,' she'd tell us. 'Eat up.' "

My old man never forgot his hardscrabble days, even long after he grew up and could afford the nice things in life. By the time I was born he knew he'd never have to worry where his next meal was coming from, but it was important to him that his sons learn the hard lessons life teaches. He wanted to make sure that I would be tough enough to survive and prosper as he had done. To him, life was one big hard lesson.

I guess the first important lesson my dad taught me was to be independent. I was just four years old when he took me out to the shopping center and left me there. I'll never forget that feeling as I watched him drive away, with just that little loving wave. A few days later, when that nice policeman brought me home, my dad and I both knew I'd learned a very important lesson.

Life on the plains, where twisters seem to spring right out of the good earth, had taught my dad how to deal with emergencies. "When you have to react real quick," he always said, "you learn the stuff you're made of." In the small town where I was raised there weren't too many opportunities to test how I would respond to unexpected problems, so he tried to help.

I'll never forget the day of my ninth birthday. Dad was driving and I was next to him in the passenger seat. Suddenly he screamed, "Think fast!" and leaped right out of the car.

I had to learn how to drive right there on the spot. But as long as I live, I'll never forget that broad, proud smile on his face when I pulled that old car up the driveway. That was my old man.

My dad also understood the value of a good sense of humor. "Back in the old days," he often told me, "we were so poor we had to beg for jokes." So sometimes, when I was fast asleep, dreaming of the home runs I would hit, he would gently lean over my bed and shout into my ear, "Russian bombers! Russian bombers! Run! Run!" And then he would laugh and laugh.

But as Dad got older and that cough became worse, he knew he wasn't going to always be there for me, and he wanted to make sure I could handle the real tough times. I was fourteen years old, I remember, when the police came to the high school to arrest me. As they booked me, they explained that "an anonymous caller" had informed them that I had held up a convenience store. I smiled. That was my old man, I knew, teaching me how to deal with adversity. But two days later he was right there to bail me out.

Oh, sometimes the lessons were hard. I sure did miss my little brother after that tragic "accident." And when my dad spent all the money I'd saved for college, it helped me learn that I could survive on almost nothing. But there wasn't one single day when I doubted his love for me.

My old man isn't here anymore, but I've never forgotten the lessons he taught me. So sometimes, late at night, when I'm sitting there on the floor, I look at my son, sleeping like an angel, and I know that one day soon I'll be taking him to the mall.

Just like my old man.

William Garvey

Struck by Luck

NO ONE CAN EXPLAIN LUCK. LUCK EITHER LAYS ITS GOLDEN hand on your shoulder or coldly passes by. Paul "Buck" Fisher was not a lucky person. Never once in his entire life had he gotten something for nothing. He'd never won a single prize or met the girl of his dreams. He even had great difficulty finding an empty space in a large parking lot. Good fortune always seemed to be just beyond his grasp.

Life for Buck Fisher became a constant struggle. He had difficulty holding a job, and he was forced to live in dilapidated housing. Finally, desperate, he turned to a life of petty crime. He began by shoplifting, then moved on to stealing handbags and after several years graduated to armed robbery. But even then, luck evaded him. In his very first attempt at armed robbery, he tried to hold up a doughnut shop frequented by police officers. When Buck pulled his toy gun from his belt and announced, "This is a stickup," the five police officers in the shop drew their weapons. In a brief burst of gunfire, Buck Fisher was shot three times in the chest.

An ambulance raced him to the hospital, where surgeons labored six hours to save his life. And there, lying in a hospital operating room, Buck Fisher's luck finally changed!

One bullet had missed his heart by less than a millimeter. Had it been the width of a fingernail closer to his heart, he would have died instantly. While the surgeon was removing that bullet, he happened to notice a bulging aneurysm—a miniature balloon ready to burst—in the aorta leading from Fisher's heart. The surgeon performed a delicate resection, inserting a synthetic graft and eliminating the danger from the aneurysm.

Had Fisher not been shot in the failed robbery attempt, within a few days at most that aneurysm would have burst, killing him. Instead, the bypass saved his life, enabling Paul "Buck" Fisher to serve every single day of his twenty-five-year sentence. Luck had found Buck Fisher in the nick of time.

I Am an Urban Teacher

- I am an urban teacher.
- I will follow the universal code of urban teachers: Cover me.
- I believe that sexual education is a subject, not an after-school activity.
- I believe that all calibers are to be treated equally.
- I am confident that someday the ringing in my ears will disappear.
- I will never accept bribes when giving report-card grades; though, I will take all threats into consideration.
- I will not consider "The Effects of Drugs on Students" an acceptable science project.
- I will always honor the memory of the vice principal for disciplinary affairs.
- I will never judge students by their race, creed, gender, or religion; only by the quality of their weapon.

- I will never carry cash during school hours.
- I will refuse to allow my chemistry students to make pipe bombs.
- I will never testify against a student.
- I will actively participate in the Parole Officers-Teachers Association.
- I will not permit students to throw food in the cafeteria while the food is still in a can.
- I will happily sell raffle books to raise funds for new batteries for the metal detector.
- I will never reply to a student's demands, no matter how outrageous, with the phrase "Over my dead body."
- I will fight fire with fire—but I will never fire first!
- I will never require my students to conjugate the verbs *to confess, to squeal,* or *to lay.*
- I will never enter the boys' room without first saying loudly, "Wait right here, Killer. I'll be right out."
- I will require all students who are absent to bring me a note from their gang leader.
- I am an urban teacher, hear my song: "Help" by the Beatles.

Susan Koenig

A Meditation for
Investment Bankers

A pessimist is someone who doesn't believe his book about torture, murder, and brutality will sell, while an optimist is someone who believes it will.

—SIR ROGER WOOLMUTH

ONE DAY I WAS FEELING SORRY FOR MYSELF BECAUSE I couldn't afford to rent a château in the south of France for the summer, until on that same day I met an investment banker who couldn't afford his own chauffeured limousine. And that investment banker had been feeling sorry for himself until he met an investment banker who couldn't afford a state-of-the-art digital sound system for his media room. And he had been feeling sorry for himself until he met an investment banker who couldn't afford to wear Armani. And she had been feeling sorry for herself until she met an investment banker who couldn't afford custom-made Loeb shoes.

But the very next day the stock market went up eleven points and all of us were able to afford all of these things that we wanted.

9

The Road Much Less Traveled

THERE WERE TWO ROUTES THAT WOULD TAKE ME TO MY BEST friend's house: the superhighway, a straight and colorless dash cut through the mountains, and the winding Old Motor Parkway, which had been all but forgotten. I always took the superhighway, and I did so without thinking. It seemed the easiest path to follow, and it was the road everyone else seemed to be taking. It was the safe route.

One day though, when my life was in turmoil, I noticed the battered sign for Route 461. Why not, I wondered, why not take the road much less traveled and see where it took me? I realized that I'd spent my life taking the safe roads, following traffic, without giving much thought to the possibilities of other paths.

So instead of once again playing it safe, I turned onto the road that held the promise of adventure. And as I drove along, I discovered many things:

There were big potholes everywhere that had never

been repaired. Thick clumps of grass were growing right through the cracked surface.

There were no signs or directions of any kind.

There were no services at all. I passed an old gas station, but it obviously had been abandoned long ago.

I had to swerve to avoid a hunk of rusting metal in the middle of the road. I think it might have been an old engine.

Much of the parkway was impassable, so I kept having to take detours.

And so, I learned an important lesson that day. There is a good reason people don't take the roads much less traveled. They're dangerous and it can take you more than twice as long to get to your destination.

From that day on, I've always taken the roads much more traveled, and I have never had to swerve to void a big rusting metal thing again.

Bruce McDonald

The Lonely Little Raindrop

LIKE MOST CHILDREN HER AGE, FIVE-YEAR-OLD LAURA VER-
tullo was terribly afraid of being left alone. To calm
her fears, her father told her this story, which had
been told to him by his father, a story that Laura has
now shared with her own children:

Once there was a tiny little raindrop who lived in
a great big cloud. The little raindrop had no friends.
He was very lonely. He longed desperately for someone to play with. And then one day, with no warning
at all, he started falling. Down, down, down he fell.
There was nothing to hold on to. What would happen
to him, he wondered, where was he going? He was
so frightened he could hardly breathe.

Softly, he landed on the ground. He was fine, but
he had no idea where he was. He looked all around
but there was nothing as far as he could see. No other
raindrops were nearby at all. Once again he was all
alone, but this time he was in a strange place. He

12

didn't know what to do. He was so cold. In his whole life, he had never felt so bad.

And then, not too far away, one more little raindrop landed. And then another little raindrop, and then another. The little raindrop was so happy. He was not alone in a strange place anymore.

All the little raindrops huddled really close together for safety, and soon they had made a little puddle. For the first time in as long as the little raindrop could remember, he had friends to play with. He wasn't scared anymore.

Soon, more little raindrops fell, then more and more and more. And slowly the little puddle turned into a tiny stream, and the lonely little raindrop and his friends started rolling along. This was the most fun the little raindrop had had in his whole entire life. He rolled happily down the street, with millions and millions of his new friends.

But still more raindrops fell, and then even more! The tiny little stream became bigger and bigger. It became a river and the little raindrop was carried along. He had so many new friends to play with. This was the best time he had ever had. And even as the little raindrop and his friends sped onward, more and more raindrops came to play with them and the river became bigger and bigger. As far as the little raindrop could see, there were millions and billions and trillions of raindrops. No raindrop had ever had so many friends.

The river of playing raindrops rolled and rolled and finally came to a great big dam! And there were so many raindrops that they rolled right over the big dam and right into the nice town. The little raindrop and all his friends were having so much fun he couldn't believe it! He rolled right through the town, knocking down everything that got in the way. He helped knock down walls and houses, he knocked down stores and schools, trees and power posts. The little raindrop was so happy. He never knew it was possible to have so much fun.

The little raindrops rolled right through the whole town and even out the other side. He played for days and days and days until he finally became very tired. He slowed down and finally, he stopped. All that playing had made him exhausted. And as he lay there with his friends, Mr. Sun came out. The lonely little raindrop could feel the warmth from the sun, and soon the most amazing thing happened. His friends got smaller and smaller and soon disappeared, floating up into the air in tiny, tiny droplets! And then he felt it happening to him. Little by little he was carried upward, back into a cloud.

But this time the little raindrop wasn't scared at all, for he knew he would never be lonely again. As he floated back into the big blue sky, he could barely wait until the next time he got to play with all of his new friends. They had all promised to get together next year and bring even more friends. And he wondered what they had meant when they asked him if he had ever heard the story of a man named Noah.

What I Learned From My Fish Tank

If you want to know if a glass is half-empty or half-full,
spill it on a woman wearing a white dress.

—Shane Darren Ehrmann

The day before my tenth birthday my father told me he had a wonderful surprise for me. I just knew it had to be that new baseball glove I wanted so desperately. Or even better, maybe it was a new slot-car racetrack with supertraction cars. I was so excited I barely slept that night.

But when I came home from school on my birthday, I found my father was in my room—setting up a fifty-gallon fish tank. Two dozen strange-colored fish were swimming around. Fish? None of my friends had a fish tank. Nobody wanted one either. Fish tanks were for parents. You can't play with fish. There was no way my friends would ever want to come over to my house to watch my fish. I smiled and tried real hard not to show my disappointment. "It's great, Dad," I said, "thanks."

But I couldn't fool Dad. "I know this isn't exactly what you wanted," he said with a grim smile, "but give it a chance. I'll bet you anything that if you do, you'll see that there's a whole world right here. All you have to do is look for it."

I promised him I would try, but inside I knew I wouldn't. Tropical fish! What a dumb gift, I thought. And for the first few days I paid almost no attention to these fish, as if ignoring them might make the tank go away. But then one night, as I was doing my homework, I found myself staring at it. The colors of the fish were amazing. They looked like they had been painted by a great painter. And they glided so smoothly through the water, smooth as a great shortstop making a play in the hole.

As the days passed, I started paying more and more attention to these fish. I watched them for hours, until I got to know them. I gave them names and learned how to care for them. And gradually, I began to understand what my father had told me: there was a whole world in that tank.

By watching my fish tank I learned so many lessons that were to prove valuable to me later in my life. I learned that what appears to be a random environment with fish just swimming around is actually a highly structured society in which the fish are dependent upon each other.

I learned the meaning of responsibility. If I didn't feed these fish or clean the water, they would not survive, so each day I would add a precise amount of food and each week I would filter the water.

I learned to appreciate the beauty of nature in all

its variety and to wonder at the existence of such strange and beautiful creatures.

I learned that a fish tank was a fragile world, and the fish faced many of the same dangers we do in our world, such as overcrowding and environmental pollution.

I learned that the biggest and strongest fish would get most of the food, which enabled them to grow even bigger and stronger and then get even more of the food.

I learned that the fish didn't care at all about the other fish, they didn't even know the other fishes' names, they have no friends, no loyalty, and it didn't seem to affect them at all.

As I got older, I noticed that they had all the sex they wanted and they didn't even have to make a date or beg or pretend to have a fatal fish disease.

And finally, I learned probably the most important lesson of all: in the end, the big fish eat the little fish.

Years later, after I graduated from law school, I found that the lessons I had learned from my fish tank could be applied to the real world. And they made all the difference in my life. So when I look back upon that gift, I understand exactly what my father meant when he gave it to me. And I know it was the greatest gift I've ever received.

A Taste of Money

In THE ANNALS OF POLITICAL HISTORY, FEW CANDIDATES FOR office have ever been as candid as New York's Thomas Robbins. A recent poll of U.S. senators voted Robbins's speech in his 1990 Senate campaign one of the five greatest political speeches of the twentieth century. Many said that his stirring words have served as an inspiration to them in their own campaigns. Here is an excerpt from that speech:

"The sad reality of politics is that politicians will do and say almost anything to raise money during a political campaign. The fact is that money does buy access to the halls of power, and the more money you give, the better access you receive. This has got to change. This is perverting our entire political system. And so I promise you, my friends, on my very first day in the Senate of the United States, I will introduce legislation to make sure that it does change. I know you will all support me in this great endeavor.

Unfortunately, getting Congress to change the way politicians raise money is an expensive proposition. It costs a lot of money. And without your financial support, it will be impossible for me to change the system. So if you're as serious as I am about changing a system where money buys power, you'll contribute to my campaign for the United States Senate.

This is a vitally important issue for the future of this country. I know many of you feel just as strongly about it as I do. So please, if you want to know how your generous contribution will help, please feel free to contact me directly. I'd be delighted to meet with you personally to discuss this or any other issues that concern you."

That day, Thomas Robbins raised $135,000 in campaign contributions.

The True Meaning of Love

I LEARNED THE MEANING OF TRUE LOVE ON A NEW YORK street corner. It was the corner of Madison Avenue and Fifty-second Street, a corner I passed each day on my way home from work. And often, coming from the opposite direction, I saw a beautiful woman. On occasion our eyes would meet as we passed, and she would demurely look away. For months neither one of us dared speak to the other.

As those months sped by, toward the end of each day, I found myself watching the clock, counting the moments until I might see my mystery woman again. I began leaving the office early and waiting a block away until I saw her in the distance, and only then would I start my walk. To my amazement, I realized I was falling in love with her.

Finally, one magnificent fall day, I summoned the courage to speak to her: "Excuse me, but my name—"

Before I could finish, she replied, "I'm sorry, but

I'm late. My husband is waiting for me." And she walked on.

She was married. I was shattered. Suddenly, the days at work seemed endless. I started walking on the other side of the street. My fantasy had been destroyed. But then, one day I realized how silly I had been. How wrong. Because she was not free to love me, I had stopped loving her. I had fallen into a terrible trap—I realized that my love for her had been dependent on her returning those feelings.

On that day, I understood true love is unconditional. I had spent too much of my life refusing to love another person until I could be sure my love would be returned. That wasn't love, I realized, it was simply a form of narcissism. The healthy expression of true love does not require anything in return.

And I was in love with her. That day I watched the clock with excitement. I raced to our corner and waited. When she passed, I turned around and followed her. I followed her through the streets, onto the subway, and all the way to a small house in Queens. And then I turned around happily and went home.

I began following her every day. And after a while I began standing across the street from her house. It didn't matter to me that she didn't love me; anyone can love a person who loves them back. I was expressing a truer love.

One freezing-cold day she saw me standing there. She came outside, adorably bundled up in a coat, and said, "Please leave."

That was the first time I realized she truly cared about my welfare. I loved her more than ever. I returned day after day. As winter turned to spring, she called the police. They warned me to stay away from her and I smiled. What kind of weak love, I wondered, would so easily be deterred by the cold hand of government? True love, I knew, could not so easily be surrendered.

A few days later a big man came out of the house— I guessed it was her husband—and punched me several times. This, I understood, was a test of my love. Too often in life I'd allowed embarrassment or discomfort to force me to hide my feelings. No more. Each blow seemed to strengthen my love for her, as they served to prove the depth of my feelings.

Oh, that silly judge who thought a piece of paper called a restraining order could so easily keep me away. If a flimsy piece of paper could stop me, then my love could not possibly be real.

Many people would have stopped after that first arrest. But those people are like I once was, dependent on the feelings of others to determine their own feelings. If my love could not survive a few weeks of separation, it wasn't really love; it was infatuation. Lust. So the day of my release I returned to her house and pitched my tent.

The gunshots did frighten me, I admit. Was it possible, I wondered, that I had fallen in love with a dysfunctional person? Was the woman I loved crazy? But once again, I knew that if I allowed her few shortcomings to change my feelings, then what I was feeling could not possibly be true love.

The most difficult test of my love came when they put me in the hospital. It's been two years now, and to be honest, at times I've wondered if I still love her.

But I know that is what they want me to think. And then I remember that true love cannot be defeated by time or distance; true love is eternal. And I know then that no matter how long they keep me locked away, no matter how long they test my resolve, the hour I am free I will return to her side.

For that is the meaning of true love.

Jack Marshall

My Race to the Light

I DIED ON THE OPERATING TABLE. I KNOW I DID, BECAUSE I saw it happening. But I was above the scene, watching the doctors frantically trying to save my life. I could hear the rapid beep-beeping of my heart. Suddenly I heard someone shout, from what seemed a great distance, "We're losing him!" Then the beeping became a single, steady tone and everything started to fade.

I found myself in a long, narrow tunnel. But in the distance, far away, I saw a beautiful white light. I started moving toward it. I could feel its warmth. I felt so safe, so beautiful. And as I got closer to the light, I saw a person dressed in white. I could almost see her face. Was it my mother? Could it be my mother? Finally, I could make out her features.

I was wrong. It was not my mother. It was my ex-wife, and she was blocking the way. "And just where do you think you're going?" she demanded in that incredibly shrill voice of hers that had made my stomach churn for so many years.

"The light"—I pointed, trying to explain—"it's so beautiful."

She shook her head. "Don't you even think about it. You're gonna stay right here until I'm finished with you. Got it? I've been waiting a long time for this. Once and for all you're gonna listen to every word I have to tell you, and I really don't give a damn if it takes forever."

"I . . . I . . ." The light was growing even brighter, and warmer, more enticing. I stepped around her and raced forward.

As her voice faded, I was practically blinded by the beauty of the light. But suddenly a man seemed to emerge from the white glare. In the distance, it looked like my father. Was it possible? Could it really be my father? He spoke to me: "Look, I'm glad you're here. I need to talk to you now." It wasn't my father. It was my former boss, George Hicker. For twenty-six years, until he finally dropped dead in his tracks, he was the slave driver who had made me do his job day and night six days a week and then took all the credit for my work. As he tried to put his arm around my shoulders, he said, "I've just got a little problem here and you're just the person who can solve it. I'll just take a little while, maybe not even a millennium. But you've got some time . . ."

The light seemed to be fading. I ran toward it, faster and faster. Another man stepped forward. He looked so familiar. Could it be my eighth-grade math teacher, the meanest man I'd ever known? Was it Mr. Bellow? I moved closer until I could see him clearly. Yes, it was, it was Mr. Bellow. And he had that same angry look on his face that I remembered so well. "*Now* you listen to me. You are going to sit right here until you figure out this problem, and I don't care if it takes the rest of eternity. I don't want to hear any more of your excuses. Do we understand each other? And when you're done with that, I have some homework for you."

I looked at the light. Suddenly it seemed much less bright, less enticing. Then I heard my ex-wife, coming closer and closer, screaming, "Just wait until I get my hands on you . . ."

I knew what I had to do. I turned around and started running away from that light just as fast as I could. Gradually, the light faded away. I was in complete darkness. I was so cold, so alone. "Where am I?" I cried.

"He's coming back," I heard a voice say, "really fast. I've got a heartbeat."

Pat Murray

Sir Winston in His Prime

DURING THE EARLY DAYS OF WORLD WAR II, AS THE NAZI hoards swept through France, Belgium, and the lowland countries, Great Britain stood alone as democracy's only hope. Many nights England's prime minister, Winston Churchill, would attempt to relieve the incredible pressure he felt of having half the population of the world depending on him to protect their lives and freedom by getting so rip-roaring drunk he could not stand up.

Late one such night, as he drained still another bottle of his favorite port, a guest at Sandhurst, Lady Elizabeth Tyson, happened upon him. "Oh, Mr. Prime Minister," she said sadly, "why must you drink so?"

With bleary eyes, Churchill glanced up at her from his position on the carpet and explained, "My dear lady, I drink to forget."

"But to forget what?"

Churchill hesitated, his eyes narrowing as he tried to concentrate. Finally he admitted, "I forget." With that, he smiled broadly, threw his arms high into the air, and shouted gleefully, "By Jove! It's working!"

Lying Up!

I CANNOT TELL A LIE. I LIE. AND ANY SUCCESSFUL BUSINESS-
man who claims that he never lies is lying when he
makes that claim. No business schools teach the secrets of lying, none of the multitude of so-called "inside" business books discuss it, and no corporate
executives dare admit it, but eventually every person
in business will have to tell a lie, and the ability to
convincingly tell the right lie at the right time in the
correct way may well make all the difference between
success and failure.

Most successful businesspeople will state flatly that
they believe lying is wrong. And when they say that,
they are simply demonstrating the skill they have perfected along the hard climb up the corporate ladder.
The fact is that mastering the art of lying is not difficult, and with proper training and practice it can become as easy as claiming business deductions for
personal expenses.

The truth is that every businessman lies. I'm not
referring to the big lies, or "politician's lies," as they

are known, but rather the day-to-day little lies that are so often required. At some point it will become necessary for every one of us to tell that small lie to customers or clients, to suppliers, to employers or employees, to co-workers. Sometimes the check really isn't in the mail, or that part won't be delivered that day, or you haven't finished the paperwork, or you simply forgot to complete a task, or you've permanently misplaced a document, or the product really isn't as good as advertised, or the sale price really isn't discounted, or you don't have precisely what the customer needs. In these and many similar situations, the ability to lie with honesty and sincerity has made the difference between success and failure in so many careers.

In my lectures I am often asked, "What is a lie?" A lie is not simply not the truth; it is much more complex than that. For example, suppose your employer asks you, "Would I lie?" When you give the only possible response to that question, "No," you know you are lying. But is it truly a lie when your job is at stake? Or is it really a lie to tell a seventy-year-old customer that the snowblower he is interested in buying will last him fifty years or you'll refund the total purchase price?

While some people might believe these are lies, I believe it is more appropriate to refer to them as "selective truths." In fact, there are many different types of lies; among them are big lies, lies of omission, and lies of commission. Here's a good tool to help you remember that: Omitting lies will affect your commission!

I recently had a conversation with one of America's

best-known businessmen about the meaning of lying. "When I exaggerate the gross receipts of my businesses, hint that I might acquire properties when in fact I have absolutely no interest in them, or hire PR people to make a big story of the fact that I don't want publicity, some people might call that lying," this captain of industry said as he looked out over Central Park from his penthouse office. "But is it really? No one gets hurt and it helps create an aura of success. If people believe you're successful, they deal with you as if you are, even if you're really deeply in debt."

"Maybe that's true, Donald," I responded, "but when does an exaggeration become a lie?"

After a thoughtful pause, he decided, "When someone else does it."

There is a word to describe the very first lie most people tell in business. That word is *résumé*. In many ways a résumé is a test of your ability to successfully create a new truth. Few employers actually believe the claims made on a résumé; much of the time they don't even care about them. They are far more interested in an applicant's skill in exaggerating or originating information that cannot easily be proved inaccurate. The quality of invention present on a résumé serves as an important indicator of an individual's ability to adapt to common business situations.

Lying in business should never be confused with morality. Customers, clients, and consumers all understand and accept that truth is subjective. For this reason, educated consumers do not object when the same sales consultant who just sold them a product based on its superior quality immediately tries to sell them the extended warranty.

But never make the mistake of underestimating the consumer. He or she fully realizes that the slogan "Truth in advertising" is simply a good advertisement for advertising. The entire history of advertising is based on the desire of the consumer to believe what he wants to be true, rather than what exists. There is no such thing, for example, as a "free gift." And no matter what their own eyes tell them, people will still fervently believe the age-old claim "No one will ever be able to tell it from your real hair!"

There is no doubt that lying in business can be dangerous. Getting caught may have serious consequences. That is why it is vital that you overcome any inherent fear of lying you may have before you have to tell that lie. Generally, your most important lies will be those required to deal with stressful situations. If you are not totally prepared to lie, that lie can be the source of terrible anxiety. And that, in turn, may result in severe physical manifestations, sweating for instance. Which is why it is necessary to get all the practice you can.

I am often reminded of the wisdom of the great actor George Burns, who once said, "The most important thing in show business is sincerity. And if you can fake that, you can get away with anything." Remember, with patience, practice, and experience, you too can master the art of lying up!

Excerpted from "Lying Up"
by Jerry Podell

A Clone Poem
by Ann Tyson

I am me, And so are wc;
And together I will always be.

(repeat first verse)

(repeat first verse)

(repeat first verse)

(repeat first verse)

(rcpcat first verse)

(repeat first verse)

(repeat first verse)

(repeat first verse)

(repeat first verse)

33

(repeat first verse)

(repeat first verse)

(repeat first verse)

(repeat first verse)

The Going-Away Present

EMMA HYDE-PRUITT COULD HAVE LIVED A LIFE OF INCREDIBLE luxury. Born into one of London's top-hat families in the 1860s, she was destined to take her place among the fashionable set at Ascot. When she was seventeen, a fabulously wealthy duke asked for her hand in marriage. But the strong-willed young woman shocked the tony set by rejecting her suitor, for she had a far more important mission in mind.

As a young girl, Emma had ridden in her carriage through the mean streets of London's slums. There she had seen the children in their tattered rags, their emaciated bodies desperate for a few morsels. She gave what monies she could as a child, but as she grew older, she knew that it would not be enough. She could feed a few children for a few days, but what she really wanted to do was change their lives. So Emma Hyde-Pruitt did what no other woman of her social standing had ever done—she attended teaching college and eventually gained her license to teach!

Day and night she would roam London's dangerous "throat-cutter" alleys, gathering groups of children to teach them to read and write. If she could educate but a few, she knew, she could provide hope for all of them.

Forsaking her fashionable life, Emma Hyde-Pruitt became a fixture in the slums. When the public learned of her noble deeds, she became one of the most beloved people in London, "the Angel of the Alleys."

Emma had but one dream for herself. As she was growing up, she would sit upon her father's knee, and he would regale her with tales of the great queens of the ocean, the fleet Atlantic liners. To sail one day aboard one of these great ships remained her lifelong wish; but with the family fortune given away to the needy, she knew that would never be possible.

Or so she thought. As Emma Hyde-Pruitt approached her fiftieth birthday, her students, young and old, began pooling their money for a grand surprise. Hundreds of them gave what pittance they could, a farthing here, half a sixpence there, but they all gave. And on the occasion of her fiftieth birthday, hundreds of people whose lives she had changed gathered around as she was given the gift of their love for her: a first-class ticket on the maiden voyage of the *Titanic*.

Christopher Winter

Use It to Lose It!

For millions of Americans, it's the one thing we can't "weight" to lose! Americans have become obsessed with dieting. We count calories, eat cabbage soup, drink diet drinks, swallow water pills, investigate food allergies, and eliminate wheat products. We try all-protein diets and no-protein diets, all-carbohydrates and no-carbohydrates, low-fat diets and low-salt diets. We spend more than $2 billion a year on crash diets, fad diets, low-salt diets, health-food diets, and medically supervised diets. And almost all of these diets have one thing in common—they provide only temporary relief from those overweight blues. As every veteran of the weight-loss wars knows, the only guaranteed way to lose pounds and keep them off permanently is to change your behavior: eat less and exercise more. But putting that into practice can sometimes be extremely difficult. Trying to help people find the means to do that served as the impetus behind Dr. Arthur Perschetz's Anxiety Diet.

Dr. Perschetz was a renowned general practitioner

serving the Wall Street community in New York City. After the stock market crash in 1987, Dr. Perschetz noticed that many of his patients had successfully lost weight and, much more importantly, were keeping it off. He wondered if there might be some correlation between the anxiety caused by the crash and this phenomenon. Might the loss of money also lead to the loss of unwanted pounds?

This theory was consistent with a trend Dr. Perschetz had already noted: his overweight patients, fat people, appeared to be consistently jovial, while his thinner patients often seemed tense, nervous, and anxious.

He decided to conduct an experiment. He told twenty-five of his patients that they were suffering from a fatal disease and had less than a year to live. And he told another twenty-five patients that they were perfectly healthy. Then he monitored both groups. The results were striking. At the end of three months, those patients who believed they were suffering from a fatal disease lost between eight and twelve pounds, while members of the control group actually gained two to three pounds.

At the end of this test Dr. Perschetz was able to tell his test group that not only did they not have a fatal disease and were not going to die, but that they had lost a minimum of eight pounds.

From this was born the famed Dr. Perschetz Anxiety Diet. "Bad things happen to each of us," he wrote in the introduction to his best-selling diet book. "The question is how to use them for positive gain. Or in this case, positive loss. Now there is a means to 'Use it to lose it!' "

Dr. Perschetz even showed readers how to create anxiety in their life when none existed. Helpful hints like "Have you checked the balance on your joint bank account lately?" "Does your boss seem to be having difficulty looking you in the eye these days?" and "Remember, even those minor aches and pains can be the first symptoms of serious disease" were offered to self-induce the kind of anxiety that quickly destroys an appetite, leading directly to weight loss!

A "diet for real life," the Anxiety Diet is now recognized as the most popular and successful diet plan in American history! All because one astute physician realized that rather than worrying about losing weight, people could lose weight by worrying!

Frank Weyman

Table Manners

THERE ONCE WAS A TIME WHEN THE FORK WAS KING OF THE Table. Proud and alone, the fork ruled his domain. And there was peace and harmony on the tabletop. Everything was fine—until the night that soup was served.

The fork could not lift the soup. He tried and tried, but there was nothing he could do. Each time he dipped into the soup, it dribbled through his long, thin tines. Finally, the spoon, the fork's oldest enemy, came along. "*I* can lift the soup," said the spoon.

Reluctantly, the fork accepted the assistance of the spoon. Together, the fork realized, they could be even more powerful. Working as a team, it seemed as if there was nothing they could not accomplish. And once again, everything on the tabletop was peaceful—until the night that meat was served.

The fork and the spoon worked together, but as hard as they tried, they could not cut the meat. Finally, the knife, the enemy of both the fork and the spoon, came along. "*I* can cut the meat," said the knife.

Reluctantly, the fork and the spoon accepted the assistance of the knife. The knife cut the meat and the fork picked it up. Together, the fork, the spoon, and the knife were all-powerful. Working as a team, there was truly nothing they could not accomplish.

And so, for a time, peace and harmony reigned on the tabletop. For it was true; working together, the fork and the spoon and the knife were able to accomplish all that was demanded of them. But then one dark night, lemon meringue pie was served. The knife said quickly, "I can cut it." The spoon said pleasantly, "And I can pick it up." But the fork said, "I can cut it *and* pick it up."

So once again, there was distrust on the tabletop. And while the spoon was busily occupied picking up the lemon meringue pie, the fork whispered to the knife, "You know, we don't really need the spoon. And if we get rid of him, there'll be more for us!" So while the spoon's handle was turned, the fork and the knife pushed him off the table.

For a time, there was an uneasy peace on the tabletop. Then one day a big piece of chocolate cake was served. Chocolate cake was the fork's favorite dessert. The fork cut into the cake and picked it up. It was delicious! And as the fork cut another piece, he realized he didn't need the knife anymore. So that night, when the knife had his blade turned, the fork pushed him off the table.

Once again, the fork was King of the Table. And there was peace and happiness. Until the very next night—when, once again, soup was served.

Robert Simon

Johnny Henderson's Amazing Discovery

Is it cold in here, or is it just me?

—'Old Man' Winter

Our most important discoveries are often made in painful ways. When Johnny Henderson was a young boy, he was small and thin. He wore thick glasses and he wasn't good at sports. The other kids in school were mean to him. They would laugh at him and call him terrible names. They would push him down and break his glasses. When they picked teams for the games, he was always the last one selected. Johnny was humiliated; he hated going to school and spent all of his free time by himself.

One day his grandfather came to visit. He noticed how sad Johnny looked and asked him what was wrong. At first, Johnny was reluctant to tell him, but then, in a torrent of tears, it all came out. Johnny told his grandpa how all the other children picked on him; he told him about the names they called him and how much he hated all of them.

His grandfather listened closely, and when Johnny was done, his grandfather dried his tears and gave him the advice that changed his life: "You know, Johnny, it doesn't matter what other people say or do or think. The only thing that's really important is how you feel about yourself. So the best thing you can do for yourself is learn how to get even with all the other kids. Believe me, nothing will make you feel better about yourself than getting even."

So Johnny listened to his "Grumps," as he called him. Two days later a girl tripped Johnny and he fell in the mud. Instead of crying about it, later that day, when that little girl wasn't looking, Johnny took all her books and soaked them through and through in the sink. And when he did that, an amazing thing happened. For the first time in his whole life, he felt proud of himself. He felt wonderful. From that day on, he dedicated himself to getting back at anyone who took advantage of him.

For Johnny Henderson, life became a big adventure. He spent a lot of his time just thinking up neat ways to get even with the other kids without getting caught. He learned how to poke holes in bike tires and add dirt to sandwiches. He made "hang-up" calls late at night and learned how to slip papers out of the pile without being seen when the teacher asked the students to pass their homework forward. And as he perfected these skills, he found that his self-esteem grew stronger and stronger. He learned how to think and plan and follow through. And he discovered that as he gained his confidence, people paid attention to him. When he got a little older, he discovered that he didn't even have to wait for people to do things to him to get even with them. He could exact revenge even before they did anything, when he knew they were planning it.

As time passed, Johnny Henderson became an expert at the art of getting even. Eventually he wanted to share what he had learned with others and founded his now famous "Getting Good and Even" seminars. John Henderson has since traveled around the world spreading his message: "Quit your grievin', it's time to get even!" More than one million people, including several world leaders, have attended his seminars, and millions more have learned from his inspirational tapes and books. John Henderson, once a tortured young man, has taught the world the value of getting even.

For as John Lawrence Henderson has truly proved, getting even is the best revenge!

Scott Whitney

The Five W's of Motherhood

MRS. JANE ROBBINS, A FORMER METROPOLITAN REPORTER for the Flint (Mich.) *Journal,* came up with an interesting concept. Why not apply the famed "Five W's" of journalism to real life? As a young reporter she had been taught that all the pertinent facts needed for a story could be learned by asking six simple questions: who, what, when, where, why, and sometimes, how. Jane Robbins realized that by asking these same questions of her teenage daughter, she could obtain all the important information any mother needs to know about her child's welfare:

Who are you going with?

What are you going to do?

When will you be home?

Where will you be?

Why don't you call me and let me know you're there?

How are you getting home?

Unfortunately, when asked these questions, her fifteen-year-old daughter, Tamara, responded with the "Five W's" of teenagers:

Who died and made you Queen of the World?

What do you want from my life?

When are you going to stop treating me like a child?

Where do you get off telling me what to do?

Why can't you just leave me alone?

How can you do this to me?

Jane Robbins abandoned her idea.

Real Therapy

I called [the psychiatrist] to make an appointment, and after we'd discussed my reasons for wanting to see him, I asked, "How much is your fee?"
"Three hundred dollars an hour," he said.
"Three hundred dollars an hour!" I couldn't believe it.
"Wow," I said, "I'd have to be crazy to pay a psychiatrist that much money."
"Neat, isn't it?" he replied, chuckling.

—LESLIE NIELSEN in his pseudography,
The Naked Truth

I STARTED THE REVOLUTION BY ACCIDENT. I HAD BEEN IN PSY-chiatric practice in New York City for almost twenty years. My technique I would describe as "impure Freudian." I believed completely in Freud's dictate that the doctor should never speak to his patient, although I often found myself debating that with my patients.

After almost two decades I had grown weary of hearing people complain. That's all they did when they came to see me. It seemed like nothing was ever good enough for them. Everybody was against them. All they could do was blame their parents or their spouse. This was the most negative group of people I had ever encountered in my life. Just listening to them was making me depressed.

My personal breakthrough came one afternoon as I sat there listening to Mr. A. Admittedly, I did not like Mr. A. He sniveled. And all he wanted to talk about was his inferiority complex. As if I really cared. But week after week, session after session, for more than three years, I had to listen to his garbage. Finally, and I don't know where this came from, when he started that infernal whining once again, I looked right at him and said forcefully, "Mr. A, you don't have an inferiority complex. You are inferior! Other people are better than you at everything. So why don't you just stop complaining about it and deal with it."

I don't know which one of us was more shocked to hear those words. Mr. A sat there stunned. Then slowly a smile spread across his face and he asked softly, "You mean I'm not crazy?"

"No," I shouted at him, "you really are inferior!"

"Thank you, Doctor. Thank you." He left my office that afternoon a happy man. I too was pleased at this unexpected outcome. What I had not been able to do in years of traditional therapy I had done in a single afternoon: I had cured his illness. And that was the day what has come to be known as Reality Therapy was born.

After this initial success, I attempted to apply the same technique to other patients. Mr. B, for example, was paranoid, living in constant fear that he was being followed. "Listen to me," I shouted at him. "You make twelve thousand dollars a year, you live in a fifth-floor walk-up, and you haven't showered in three weeks. Believe me, no one is following you! Do you understand? Nobody cares!"

Mr. B was startled. Although it was difficult for him to surrender his fantasy, he could not deny the truth. He left my office cured of his paranoia.

This confrontational technique rapidly proved successful with the majority of my patients. Mr. C suffered from an obsessive-compulsive disorder and would wash his hands as often as fifty times a day. During our weekly session I was able to tell him, "The truth is, Mr. C, you're crazy."

"You mean, you mean . . . my hands really aren't dirty?"

"No, they're clean as a whistle. You're just nuttier than a fruitcake."

As was the case with most of my patients, he seemed quite relieved to learn the truth about his condition. It also quickly became apparent that the more honest I was with them, the more free I became. Reality Therapy was working: I felt better than I had in years.

Obviously, each patient required highly personalized Reality Therapy. Mr. D, for example, had spent many years with me trying to resolve his masochism. And frankly, I was bored listening to him. As he droned on and on, I suddenly went over to him and punched him as hard as I could in the stomach. "You big boring bag of wind," I shouted at him, "how'd you like that?"

He shriveled in fear. "I . . . I didn't," he said, then

realizing what he had said, repeatedly loudly, "I didn't like it at all. I hated it! I'm cured."

Unfortunately, I found that some cases proved too complex to be solved with Reality Therapy and required more intensive treatment. Mr. E and Ms. F was a rare bisexual schizophrenic, who did not get along with him or herself. He was unhappy, constantly arguing over the smallest things like who should clear the table after dinner. I tried many strategies, suggesting he sleep in separate bedrooms or go on separate vacations, but nothing helped. Finally I recommended couples counseling.

I did not anticipate the controversy that Reality Therapy would create. Certain patients do not respond well to confrontation. When confronted with reality, they tend to take drastic action, and in extreme cases they will resort to consulting another therapist. So I must emphasize that in the hands of an improperly trained Reality Therapist there is substantial risk. But properly administered, this is a treatment that can and has improved life for many unhappy psychiatrists.

Dr. Jeremy Mullis

The Greatest Man in History

SOME MEN CHOOSE TO MAKE A DIFFERENCE IN LIFE. OTHERS choose to stand idly by. This is the story of an extraordinary man who has dedicated his life to bringing joy to other people. A man willing to use his own incredible reputation to help others. A man unlike any other man of good taste and fine bearing who has ever lived. It is the story of the incredible legend, the one, the only, King of all Media, Mr. Howard Stern.

Howard Stern's unbelievable success was built on honesty and risk taking. One day the amazing Howard Stern came upon a small book of humorous stories about the foibles of life. It was a small book, much like the book you are holding in your hands right now, in fact. Same size, same cover, same stories. The book was selling nicely, the reviews had been splendid, but it was not a best-seller. At least not until the incredibly wonderful, unbelievably talented, handsome radio, publishing, television, and movie star Howard Stern discovered it and decided to bring it to the attention of his listeners.

CHICKEN POOP FOR THE SOUL

In that beautiful voice of his, the brilliant, zany star-actor-comedian told his listeners in his unique, hilarious style how much he had enjoyed this small book, similar in every way to the book you are now reading. His listeners, the single, finest, most loyal group of human beings ever to gather at the feet of a genius, followed the suggestion of the wise and wonderful sovereign of the airwaves, Mr. Howard Stern, and purchased this small, but endearing book, which included exactly the same stories as in the book you are holding.

With little more than a few words, the all-powerful Master of the Media, to whom each supporter of the First Amendment and, in fact, the entire American way of life owes the deepest and most humble gratitude, had turned this little book into a best-seller. Exercising his amazing influence, this prodigious humanitarian was single-handedly responsible for the attention the book received. Out-oprahing even the lovely and beautiful and kind Ms. Winfrey, the decent, righteous, benevolent, generous, handsome, incredibly sexy, intellectual Stern, who grew up on Long Island as did the author of this book similar to the one you are now holding, managed to change the author's life in only a few brief seconds of valuable radio time. And while those few seconds meant almost nothing to the uniquely clever, witty Mr. Howard Stern, they meant everything to the author of the book similar to the one you are now holding. In hardly more time than the blink of an eye, the big-hearted, big-other-body-parts, munificent, kind and noble, much beloved Howard Stern had proven simply by mentioning the book, which was so similar to the one you are now reading, or even reading one small passage from it, that he could turn it into a bestseller. That he is, truly and without doubt, Mr. King.

Incredibly, however, if the good and gracious Howard Stern had not found this book, published by the same publisher who published this book, the incredibly wonderful genius, the inimitable original, hilariously funny Don Imus was ready to do exactly the same thing.

David Jay Fisher

Take a Moment to Remember

AT THOSE TIMES WHEN YOU'RE FEELING INSECURE, INEPT, AND unsuccessful, when it seems as if every person you know is more successful and accomplished than you are, it's important to take a moment to remember that:

Alexander the Great, who conquered the world before his thirtieth birthday, did not graduate from high school!

Plato, considered by many to be the greatest philosopher in history, never read a single book!

William Shakespeare, the greatest writer in history, did not know how to type!

Christopher Columbus, the man who sailed across uncharted oceans in a tiny wooden sailing ship to discover America, never drove a car!

John D. Rockefeller, once the richest man in the world, was never approved for a credit card!

Knute Rockne, the legendary Notre Dame football coach, never won a single NCAA championship!

Amadeus Mozart, perhaps the greatest composer in history, did not even own a radio!

In his entire lifetime, not a single article about Leonardo da Vinci, one of the greatest scientists and artists in history, ever appeared in a major magazine!

And Benjamin Franklin, the legendary statesman and inventor, never successfully programmed his own VCR!

Ted Webb

Timmy Johnson's Last Wish

LITTLE TIMMY JOHNSON WAS A VERY SICK BOY. THE DOC-
tors had tried hard, but they could do nothing more
to help him. Timmy wasn't scared, but he had one
wish. He wanted to receive postcards from all over the
world, more postcards than anyone else had gotten in
his whole life; enough postcards to get him into the
Guinness Book of World Records, where he would live
forever and ever.

When his mom told a reporter for the local newspaper, the *Clarion*, they printed a big story on the front
page. Only 780 people lived in Mapletown, but just
about every one of them mailed a postcard to little
Timmy. They sent hundreds and hundreds; picture
postcards and funny postcards, postcards from far-
away places like Nebraska, postcards with a picture of
a dog pulling down a baby's diaper. The second-grade
class even made postcards from shirt cardboard for
Timmy. There were so many postcards that poor Mrs.
Peterson, who ran the local post office, was just about

overwhelmed. And the mailman, old Mr. Burns, who had carried the mail on his aching back for forty years, could barely even lift his mailbag.

But still little Timmy was very sad. Hundreds of postcards were not nearly enough to earn him a place in the *Guinness* book. And just when he was about to give up, a producer on the *ABC Evening News* heard about Timmy's plight and decided to help him. That night Peter Jennings told the nation about Timmy's last wish, and the very next day postcards began arriving. Hundreds of postcards, then thousands, then tens of thousands arrived every day. Newspapers and magazines carried the heartwarming story, and even more postcards arrived. More postcards than anyone had ever imagined arrived from every state, and then they began coming from Europe and Asia and even little islands in the Pacific Ocean that no one ever knew existed.

There were so many postcards nobody knew what to do with them. Old Mr. Burns tried to deliver a sackful one day and made it about fifty feet from the post office before he keeled over and died. Mrs. Peterson lasted almost a month before the stress got her and they had to put her in the loony home. With so many postcards arriving daily no other mail could get through. Bills weren't delivered so they couldn't be paid causing hundreds of people in town to lose their phone service and electricity. The most terrifying words anyone had ever heard became "The check is in the mail." Stores couldn't bill their customers or reach them by phone, so within three months most of the shops on Main Street had to shut their doors.

And still the postcards continued to arrive by the

tens of thousands. It was the most mail anyone had ever gotten. People from all over the world were trying to fulfill little Timmy Johnson's last wish. It made them all feel so good.

With the town pretty much shut down, except for the convoys of big mail trucks that roared down Main Street all day and night, people started packing up and leaving. Families that had lived happily in Mapletown for generations boarded up their homes and left. Mapletown became a ghost town.

But then, an amazing thing happened. A miracle, some people said. Little Timmy woke up one morning and his pain was gone. He could breathe easily. The doctors attributed his incredible recovery to his joy at receiving more postcards than anyone else in history and earning his place in the *Guinness* book. Little Timmy Johnson was cured!

The news of his recovery spread slowly, so the postcards continued to arrive. No one could stop it. By that point the town was pretty much deserted and Timmy had no one to play with. So each day he would try to climb to the top of his postcard mountain, which continued to grow and grow and grow. Eventually it was estimated that Timmy had received 12 million postcards from every state and more than ninety countries around the world!

All traces of his disease seemed to have disappeared. But sometimes fate is not so kind. The disease had simply been in brief remission. One morning he awoke and it had returned. A few days later, Little Timmy peacefully passed away. His doctors reported that he had died with a smile on his face, knowing that he would live forever in the *Guinness Book of World Records.*

As the news of Little Timmy Johnson's death spread around the world, the deluge of postcards ended. A few days later the citizens of Mapletown began returning. Once again, people dreamed of living there. They took the boards off their homes and reopened the stores. Mapletown was slowly beginning to come back to life.

And then the first condolence card arrived.

A Work in Progress

DAY AFTER DAY, OFTEN SEVEN DAYS A WEEK, JIM KLUR-
feld worked incredibly long hours. His job was his life,
and he found little time to spend with his family or
for recreation. He couldn't even enjoy the rare moments of relaxation he had because he felt too guilty
about not working. But early one morning, while
reading the newspaper on his way to work, he was
amazed to see his lifestyle and feelings described perfectly by "Dear Abby." He was a "workaholic," she
wrote, and then she described the potential consequences of that behavior.

Jim Klurfeld was thrilled and surprised to learn that
he wasn't alone, that thousands of other people had
also unwittingly become slaves to their jobs. That
morning Jim Klurfeld realized his life was slipping
away and vowed to change.

Klurfeld was surprised to discover that while thousands of people suffered from this same problem,
there was no organization to which they could turn

for help. So he decided to create one. Workaholics Anonymous, a support group, would be modeled on the twelve-step programs that have proven to be so successful fighting alcoholism and drug addiction.

Klurfeld threw himself completely into this task, devoting every spare minute he could to putting together his organization. Gradually he found himself spending less and less time at his job so he could work on this program. Early in the morning and late at night, weekends and holidays, he worked to create an organization to help people free themselves from an addiction to working. He dedicated his life to this job; he skipped meals, he rarely saw his friends, he even had to quit the company bowling team.

Finally, he was ready to schedule the very first meeting of Workaholics Anonymous. Unfortunately, it was almost impossible to find a date and time that was convenient for the people who wanted to attend. And then on the night of that meeting, every one of the people who had promised to be there had to cancel because they had too much work to do.

That failure only caused Klurfeld to redouble his efforts. After that night he began working even harder in his effort to help himself and others like him from working so hard. The first meeting of Workaholics Anonymous has not yet been rescheduled.

The Thoughts of the Longest-Distance Runner

WHEN AMERICAN LONG-DISTANCE RUNNER ALEX JORDAN DE-cided to run nonstop from coast to coast to raise awareness of knee and joint diseases, many people believed the task he had set for himself was impossible. But as Jordan persisted, state after state, his saga captured the attention of the public and became a symbol of American determination. What thoughts passed through his mind as he ran the tortuous route across the country? Using a state-of-the-art Nagma lightweight tape recorder, Jordan shared his thoughts during his run into history. Here is an excerpt from those tapes, made as he raced across Kansas:

This is really, really stupid. My feet are killing me. I've done some dumb things in my life, but where this stupid idea— Ow! Damn, that hurts. What am I, out of my mind? How did I let them talk me into this . . . I swear, if this doesn't get me on *Letterman* . . . Hey! Watch it with that truck, jerk. I swear, if I ever finish this thing . . .

Random Acts

BRIAN MCLANE HAD READ WITH FASCINATION ABOUT THE random-acts-of-kindness movement that had spread across the nation. For absolutely no reason, people were doing nice things for strangers. According to these stories, committing random acts of kindness made them feel good about themselves. Brian McLane was not a happy person, so he decided to try it: One night, for example, he was in a bar and he bought a drink for a complete stranger, a woman he had never seen before. But within a few minutes, she left alone. A few days later a store cashier gave him too much change, and rather than risk embarrassing her in front of the store manager, he kept the money. In a restaurant the woman sitting behind him left her pocketbook hanging wide open on the back of her chair and he didn't take her wallet.

But none of these things made him feel better about himself. Deep inside, he still felt angry and alienated. He still yelled at his family and friends for no reason.

One day, though, as he walked down a New York street, he suddenly felt a strong urge to kick over a garbage pail. With one strong kick he sent it careening down the block. And as he watched the garbage being strewn all over the sidewalk, he felt a wave of satisfaction flow through his entire body. For the first time in months, he felt good about himself. In fact, he felt strong and powerful.

Brian McLane had committed his very first random act of hostility.

The next day, as he strolled down the same New York street, for absolutely no reason he snapped in half the antennas on five different cars! And doing so without taking credit made him feel wonderful. A few hours later he knocked over a pile of newspapers in front of a candy store, and the warm glow he felt as he watched the wind blow papers all over the street convinced him he'd discovered something quite special. And this was the beginning of the random-acts-of-hostility movement.

Once Brian McLane discovered how good being bad made him feel, he couldn't stop. On trains he would forcibly squeeze into a space between two people that was much too small, then play his radio as loud as possible. In movie theaters he would shout out the identity of the killer in the middle of the picture. In restaurants he'd spill drinks on people, and he just loved calling up strangers in the middle of the night.

These random acts made him feel like a different person. Even his family and friends noticed the difference in him. He had become so nice they wondered what was wrong. Eventually, Brian McLane shared the secret of his happiness. Initially many people objected. It wasn't nice, they pointed out.

That was exactly the point, Brian McLane said. Reluctantly, people tried it. At first it was difficult; most people had spent so long following the laws they had forgotten how to be bad. But it quickly came back. And after their first few random acts of hostility, many people found themselves enjoying a sensation they hadn't experienced in years: they were free to be bad! And it felt just great. The simple act of kicking over a garbage pail was the most liberating thing many people had experienced in years. It changed their lives, giving them an outlet for all their frustrations, making them happier with themselves and easier to be with at home and at work.

Brian McLane hadn't set out to change the world when he committed that first simple random act of hostility. But from that small piece of garbage, his movement has spread across the world!

David Williams

The Wisdom of the Streets

Any old saying looks more profound when written in italics.

—JESSE STEVENS

AT MOST WE SPEND ONLY A FEW MINUTES WITH THEM—BUT often we walk away with knowledge that will stay with us a lifetime. For they are America's taxi drivers, the philosophers of the common man. They are men like Brooklyn's Saul Wolfe, who has observed the human condition in all of its glory and decay from the seat of his yellow cab for more than thirty-eight years. "I seen it all in my day," Wolfe admits. "You name it, I seen it right there in my backseat. I've seen the best of people and the worst."

The lifetime of experience he has put on his meter has given Saul Wolfe a unique perspective on the world. When asked what conclusions he

6 8

had reached about human nature, the wise old hack leaned back and said philosophically, "Just one. No matter how often you tell people, they're still gonna open the door on the side of the oncoming traffic."

Peter Hayman

The Joys of Depression

WHILE NORMALLY HAPPY AND ENERGETIC, LIKE MILLIONS OF other people I suffered from occasional bouts of depression. When I got depressed, I felt like a complete failure, like my whole world was collapsing. It was a terrible feeling, but I assumed that I could do nothing except wait to come out of it.

One day, though, as I bused to work in the midst of a deep depression, an elderly man struggled onto the bus and settled into the empty seat next to me. This man seemed to be as happy as I was unhappy. He was softly whistling popular standards to himself and smiling broadly, as if bemused by some wonderful secret. Finally, I could resist no longer. "Excuse me, sir," I asked, "but you seem to be so happy. Can I ask you why?"

"Oh," the man replied, "I'm not happy at all. Everything in my life has gone wrong. I have no money, no place to live, my children don't speak to me. I don't even know where my next meal is coming from. The truth is, I'm terribly depressed."

I was confused. This man seemed to be happy that he was depressed. "But if you're so depressed," I asked, "why do you appear to be so happy?"

The old man smiled, then explained, "Oh, that. You see, I learned a long time ago that being depressed can be a wonderful thing. Because if you're never depressed, how can you know when you're happy?"

I was shocked by the old man's wisdom. As I sat there on the crosstown bus, I suddenly understood that happiness was a comparative thing. If I was never depressed, I'd never have anything to compare it to, so I couldn't possibly enjoy being happy!

I got off that bus a different person. I'd always thought of depression as something negative, something to be avoided whenever possible. But suddenly I realized how little I'd appreciated this misunderstood emotion. It wasn't depression that was making me feel bad, I was feeling bad because I was depressed. If I could only learn how to be happy when I was depressed, I'd never have to worry about it again. I needed to stop trying to resist depression and instead welcome it as an old friend: Hello, depression!

From that moment on depression had an entirely new meaning for me. The more I got depressed, the happier I knew I could be. Instead of avoiding people when I was depressed, I began seeking them out. And in response to their polite question "How you feeling?" I'd gleefully reply, "I'm depressed!"

Every day, in every way, I began to change. The more I embraced depression, the happier I became when I was depressed. After a time I even began to seek out reasons to be depressed. I started hanging out around hospitals; sometimes I'd sneak into the funerals of people I didn't know. Although I'd never been a gambler, I began betting long shots and thrilled to the sadness of losing. I found the courage to pursue women I knew would not go out with me—and found happiness in being turned down by them.

As time passed, like that happily sad old man on the bus, I began to share my little secret with my friends. I taught them that being depressed does not have to mean being unhappy. And one by one, as they gave up their preconceived conceptions, they too began to discover the joys of depression.

Now, we often get together to share our saddest stories, our most unhappy moments, knowing that through our depression we have found real happiness.

The truth is, as I have learned, depression doesn't have to be . . . depressing. It is simply the other side of happiness.

Rodney Farber

A Flight of Heroes

On December 17, 1993, at a ceremony at Kitty Hawk, North Carolina, commemorating the ninetieth anniversary of the Wright brothers' first controlled flight of an engine-powered aircraft, astronaut Joseph Verola's brief speech vividly brought to life the glorious history of aviation:

"They were truly the wind beneath our wings. They were the magnificent men in their flying machines, the pioneers of aviation who risked their lives and limbs to create the air and space industry. These were the gallant men who soared into the sky in rickety contraptions held together with baling wire, not for money or fame, but simply for the love of flying. Today we take for granted the miracle of flight, but it was the courage of the brave men whom we honor here today, men who will live forever in aviation history, that made it all possible.

"Years before Wilbur and Orville Wright got their engine-powered flier off the ground in 1903, inventors were employing unusual methods to break the bonds of gravity. Among the bravest of them all was a young man from the Bronx, New York. People laughed when he proposed a tightly-wound-rubber-powered craft, but that didn't stop Ward 'Crash' Calhoun from attempting to take to the air from the edge of a mountain cliff, and in so doing gaining fame as America's first airplane-crash fatality!

"Early aviators long debated the advantages of landing on hard ground or softer water. Only two years after the Wright brothers' flight, the first attempt to land a powered aircraft on water was made by Jonathan 'Glub Glub' Boswell, who proved conclusively that airplanes do not float!

"Landing an airplane at night was considered an especially daring feat, and the honor of making the first attempted night landing is credited to the brave Parisian Olivier 'French Toast' Beytout.

"From the moment powered craft were airborne, pilots were extending the envelope, trying to reach the outer limits. Among those was one of the world's first test pilots, the first man to attempt an upside-down 'Immelmann loop' in an open cockpit, Michael 'Flathead' Bestler.

"The development of flight controls, the flaps and rudders, which give the pilot the ability to steer his craft, was a vitally important aspect of aviation progress. A lot of the early experimentation took place among the jagged cliffs of Colorado's Rocky Mountains. It was there that Chistopher 'Cup o' Bones' Spencer proved the necessity of these controls.

"Long before Col. Billy Mitchell proved that airplanes could be landed on ships at sea, daredevil pilots were trying to do just that. The very first recorded attempt was made as early as 1906 by Billy 'Sharkbait' Madden, and from that failed attempt came the knowledge that the plane must be moving faster than the ship!

"Certainly the incredible advances in improving the safety of highly volatile aviation fuel could not have been possible without the sacrifices of George 'Extra Crispy' Zelma.

"The success of engine-powered, rigid-winged aircraft did not stop development of other types of flying machines. Only months after the Wright brothers' success, the first attempt to fly a steam-powered hot-air balloon to Europe over the Atlantic Ocean ended tragically for pilot Beau 'Pop' Charles.

"The star performers of early aviation shows were the stuntmen and women, and perhaps the most famous of the 'wing-walkers' was Tyler 'Peg Legs' Ehrman. Not to be outdone, the first person to actually attempt to wing-walk on a helicopter rotor blade was the aviatrix Joanne 'L'il Bits' Curtis.

"The quest for aircraft that fly higher and faster, that can take off or land in difficult conditions, has never ended. It took many years and many failed attempts, for example, to successfully develop a plane that can take off vertically. The very first test of a plane that did not need a runway to take off resulted in a flight lasting a total of seventy feet, sixty of them straight up, in a craft piloted by the legendary Donald 'Corkscrew' O'Brian!

"The concept of jumping out of an airplane and landing safely was a dream of all early aviators, and we salute those brave pioneers of the parachute, particularly the very first man to leap from a plane to test the ability of a sheet of silk to slow his descent, Sean 'Splat' Kelly.

"And finally, the commercial aviation industry could not exist today if not for the tireless efforts of so many people to establish methods to keep our skies safe, but foremost among those people was the founder of America's air traffic control system, Bill 'Bang Bang' Garvey.

"It is these people we honor here today. I am very pleased to unveil this statue commemorating their efforts, sculptor Frederick Rappoport's *Lead Skies.*"

Richard Soll's Incredible List

In 1975, FIVE-YEAR-OLD RICHARD SOLL RECEIVED AN ASSIGN-ment from his kindergarten teacher. With the help of a parent, he was to write down ten goals he hoped to accomplish by his twenty-first birthday.

Young Rich Soll was determined to compile his list all by himself. Printing neatly, in pencil, and carefully checking the spelling of words he did not know in the new dictionary given to him by his grandmother, he painstakingly completed this list.

Twenty-two years later, while going through his personal papers, Dr. Richard Soll came across this kindergarten assignment. He smiled broadly. Though he had completely forgotten about the list, he was amazed to discover that he had accomplished each of the ten goals he had set for himself so long ago.

Reprinted here with the doctor's permission is five-year-old Richard's list:

1. Stay up until 10 P.M.

2. Sleep with all the lights out in my room.
3. Learn to ride a two-wheeler without training wheels.
4. Don't go to school.
5. Stay home without a baby-sitter.
6. Watch any TV show I want to watch.
7. Save $25.
8. Drive a real car.
9. Don't be afraid to look under my bed.
10. Eat ten pieces of gum at the same time.

Breaking Down the Bars

WHILE WORKING FOR THE DEPARTMENT OF SOCIAL SERVICES, Rosemary Rogers spent countless hours inside prisons. She was struck by the gray harshness of life behind bars, a life for many inmates that was completely devoid of beauty. Believing that brutality breeds only more brutality, she wondered if bringing the beauty and grace of poetry into inmates lives might enable at least some of them to connect with a lost part of their soul. And so Rosemary Rogers's No Bars to Expression project was born.

Rogers's plan initially received considerable opposition from experienced members of the penal system. But she persisted, using corporate donations to purchase poetry books, paper, and manual typewriters for prisoners. The results have been outstanding. Through the No Bars to Expression program, many prisoners have found an important means to express their most intimate feelings. Their poetry has been awarded numerous prizes in competitions throughout the country, and a book of their poems, *Brutal Bars of Thine*, has been published.

Three of the award-winning poems appearing in that book, each of them produced behind bars by former members of brutal gangs, follow:

My Heart Is Locked Up
by #1647594847-010

O, this place really sucks;
the warden is a jerk, jerk, jerk
the food tastes like crap
but i can make great license plates now.

Another Day Goes By
by Ali Akbar Goldberg

There goes another day. Bye bye day!
I sat in my cell a LOT OF TIME!
Then I watched some TV!
It was pretty boring!
This joint definitely ain't jumping.
There goes another day. Bye bye day!
Only 10,391 more to go!

If I Had To Do It All Over Again
by 'e'

I sit here, surrounded by walls, thinking
    thoughts.
If I had to do it all over again, oh boy, I would
    do so many things differently.

First. I'd never use that jerkoff Johnny P.
    as the lookout.
Then I would definitely hire a getaway driver
    who wouldn't get lost on the friggin'
    Long Island Expressway.
And I'd never plea-bargain after O.J.'s trial.

If I had to do it all over again.

The Secrets of Unhappiness

WHAT'S BOTHERING YOU? THAT'S WHAT THE GOVERN-
ment decided to find out when it launched a $10-
million study, "The Primary Causes of Unhappiness,"
in 1994. Mental-health professionals throughout the
country conducted more than six thousand interviews
during which subjects were asked to list those problems causing them the most concern and worry. The
recently released results of this government study
found that the primary cause of mental distress in this
nation is government studies.

Almost 80 percent of all respondents indicated that
information provided to them by government studies
had three or more times been the cause of significant
distress and had caused them to alter behavior that
they had previously enjoyed.

Most subjects reported that they had been happy or
relatively happy with their lives until learning of the
dangers that they faced. For example, more than 85
percent of all persons interviewed for this study

claimed they had little or no knowledge of the existence of the ozone layer until being informed that it might be disappearing, and they had previously never been concerned about it at all. A similarly high percentage of respondents reported having little or no concern about global warming causing rising tides until made aware of this by government studies.

The general unhappiness caused by government studies reached into the home and workplace. Almost 100 percent of all persons interviewed reported that they had never or almost never been concerned about using microwave ovens, cellular telephones, or living in proximity to power lines until government studies raised issues of potential dangers.

In particular, respondents reported that they had suffered depression, worry, anxiety, and general unhappiness after reading government studies concerning the effects on their health of the most commonly enjoyed foods. According to this study, at least half the people queried had given up or significantly decreased their consumption of the foods they most enjoyed. They had reduced intake of most sugar-based products, particularly chocolate, as well as most fried foods, foods containing saturated fats, foods grown or raised on farms using pesticides or chemical fertilizers, and foods resulting from any form of genetic engineering. They had also significantly reduced or eliminated drinks containing sugar or caffeine. They reported being fairly to very upset by government studies indicating that sugar was potentially dangerous while sugar substitutes were potentially even more dangerous.

Conversely, the respondents had significantly increased consumption of foods whose taste they most often described as "poor to cardboard."

The study also found that those people interviewed had moderately to significantly changed their normal behavior patterns due to government studies. In many cases they reported that they had reduced time spent on "enjoyable" activities, including watching television, while increasing the amount of time spent on "less enjoyable" activities, such as exercise.

The government study concluded that the elimination of government studies might significantly improve the mental health of citizens. But it also recommended that further studies be funded to consider the consequences of such an action.

The Gift of Love

THE GIFT OF LOVE CAN BE EXPRESSED IN MANY WAYS. THIS was the lesson learned by seventeen-year-old Valton Zelma and his sixteen-year-old girlfriend, Heaven. They had met in Denver at a rock concert featuring the group Raining Dead Bodies and fallen in love at first sight. They had hitchhiked to New York and joined a squatters commune in a ramshackle East Village tenement. Valton was determined to be a great tattoo artist someday, while Heaven dreamed of being a holistic midwife, but both of them worked hard begging on the mean streets of Manhattan.

As Christmas approached, each of them desperately wanted to find a gift for the other that would truly express the depth of their love. But Valton had less than ten bucks in the pocket of his dirty pants, and Heaven had little more than seventeen dollars in small change. As the snow laid a gentle blanket over the streets of New York City, each of them despaired of being able to afford a Christmas present for their loved one.

But one day, as Valton begged in Midtown, he looked in the window of a jewelry store and knew instantly that he had found the perfect gift. Nothing, he knew, would make Heaven happier than for him to be happy. He knew she would be overjoyed if he bought the solid-gold nose ring he had always wanted. So with the last few dollars of credit on his MasterCard, he bought the nose ring and had it inserted. If they really needed money, he knew, Heaven still had credit left on her Visa card.

As Heather walked sadly down another street in a different part of town, she too passed a shop and knew she had found the perfect gift for her love. Nothing, she knew, could make him happier than her having the grunge haircut she had always wanted, complete with his name stenciled into her sidewall. So with the last few dollars remaining on her credit card, she bought him this haircut for herself. If they really needed money, she knew, Valton still had credit left on his MasterCard.

When they saw each other for the first time in the dim candlelight later that night, they stood silently. For words could not express how profoundly touched each of them was by the sacrifice made by the other in the name of love.

And later, as they walked through the Christmas snowstorm, Heaven laid her bald head on his shoulder and whispered, "How we gonna pay the credit card bills?"

With love and devotion in his voice, Valton smiled

and replied, "We don't have to. We're minors. It's their fault for giving us the cards."

She nestled closer and kissed him gently on his nose ring. And then she said with love in her voice, "Maybe we can get new gas station credit cards."

Kathleen Fuller

A Taste of Freedom

One of the few political issues on which there exists almost unanimous consensus is the need to protect free speech and expression. A recent poll of U.S. senators voted an impassioned 1993 speech by Sen. Joseph Cowart (D, Maryland) on the importance of the First Amendment one of the five greatest political speeches of the twentieth century. Here is an excerpt from that speech:

"Nothing, absolutely nothing, is more vital to the preservation of our freedom than protecting the right of all people to express themselves freely and openly, without fear of government reprisal. Freedom of speech and expression is the bedrock on which this great nation was built. Our founding fathers felt that the protection of this fundamental freedom was so important that they made it the first amendment to the Constitution. For without it we would be subject to the whims of the kings.

"I stand before you today to sound the alarm that

there are people who would threaten this freedom. Let me say loud and clear that there are groups who would take away from you your freedom to express your thoughts and ideas. And they would do so in the guise of protecting your freedom.

"My fellow Americans, if we are to preserve the precious freedom to speak and think freely, we must take action to stop these people from spreading their propaganda. We cannot allow them to continue using television and radio, books and magazines, to sow fear and mistrust. In a truly free America, there is no place for people like this. I urge you to write to your elected representatives and demand that he or she take immediate action to keep these groups from polluting our media with their far-out ideas. If we are to maintain our freedom, we must guard it fiercely against those people who would take it away!

"Remember, my friends, the right of free expression is our most precious gift. It is our duty as Americans to protect that freedom for our children and our children's children. But if we fail to take action now, if we fail to stop these people right now from spreading their vicious propaganda, we will have failed in our patriotic obligations. My fellow Americans, we simply cannot allow these people to continue to preach openly against freedom of speech.

"As we have all learned, our freedom is much too precious for us to allow it to be misused. Thank you very much."

Mom's Lessons

WE ARE BORN, EACH OF US, SMALL MOUNDS OF CLAY TO BE shaped gently with delicacy and infinite care. For it is within the hands of the sculptor to create a masterpiece. And so we move through life as the embodiment of that artist's power. Few people have written as movingly about the "artisan of their soul" as Martha Stewart. In her autobiography, *We, Martha*, she lovingly recalls her artist at work:.

I always waited patiently until mother had but a few scraps of food arranged in color-coordinated piles on her plate before asking politely, "Momma, may I go and play now?"

She gently brushed her lips with a hand-embroidered napkin before responding. This was our little game. "Martha dear," she'd respond, "have you finished all of your homework?"

"Yes, Momma," I replied, "every bit of it."

"And you've made your bed?"

"Yes, with hospital corners."

"And picked up your toys?"

"I did."

"And cleaned your room?"

"I did, Momma."

"And did you stencil little flowers on all the molding?"

'I did."

"Did you gather eggs from ten different breeds of chicken and handpaint them?"

"I did, yes."

"And did you cook a three-course dinner using only organic greens gathered from your garden?"

"Uh-huh."

"And did you finish painting that faux Oriental rug on the floor?"

Fortunately, I had. "I did, Momma."

"And did you weave herringbone nests for the birdhouse?"

"Yeah, I did."

"Did you cure the gravlax, recane the kitchen chairs, gild the pumpkins, and dry the delphiniums?"

I nodded.

"Did you prepare your compost heap, make the parsnip puree, bronze the beehive, and fire the forty-piece setting of bone china?"

"I did, yes, Momma."

She paused, then smiled. "Did you find a cure for cancer this afternoon?"

I sighed, "No, Momma, I didn't. I forgot."

Her smile disappeared. "Oh, Martha, dear, whatever are we to do with you?" She took a deep breath. "You know what that means, don't you? You'll have to go to bed without your tatting shuttle."

"Yes, Momma," I said sadly, knowing that there would be no knitting for me that night. I knew the night would pass slowly, but I had learned my lesson. Secretly, though, I wondered if it might be possible to play with my new potter's wheel underneath the hand-quilted covers.

This Old House

THE OLD HOUSE ISN'T TOO MUCH TO LOOK AT ANYMORE. THE shutters are off their hinges and the roof is missing a lot of shingles; some of the windows are cracked and the wooden boards are desperate for a new coat of paint. But to me, it's still beautiful, the most beautiful house in the world.

No matter what anyone tells you, a house isn't made of brick and wood, it's made of memories, and as I look around this old house in which I grew up, the memories come flooding back into my mind. There, right in the center of the living room, there's the bare spot on the rug where our big old dog, Spot, used to settle in for the night. Spot's spot, we used to call it. And just a few feet away, behind the couch, there's my secret hiding place, the place I would hide every night when I heard Dad stumbling home from the bar.

Everywhere I look I see memories. To my adult eyes the room I shared with my sister seems so small, but once it seemed like the biggest room in the world. Coats of paint have long since covered the walls, but in my mind as I look at those walls, I can still see the messages my sister used to write to Satan.

Oh, how many hundreds of hours did I spend sitting at the old kitchen table doing my homework as Mom cooked dinner? When I run my fingers over the wall, I can still feel the plaster filling the bullet holes Dad made when he accidentally fired a clip from the semiautomatic weapon that he didn't know was loaded. Boy, until that day I never knew Mom could move so fast. Dad was so embarrassed when he got sobered up. We all laughed at that one, except Spot, of course. Poor old Spot.

As I climb the creaky old wooden staircase, I can't help but remember all the games we played there. If I look at the steps real closely, I can still see traces of the skid marks left by Grandma's wheelchair as she tried to put on the brake. Mom sure didn't think Roll Grandma Down the Stairs was a funny game. Well, we couldn't play it without Grams anyway. Poor old Grandma.

Walking into the tiny room Dad built for Grandma and Grandpa, I have to remember to duck so I don't bang my head against that low ceiling beam. How we used to laugh every time we heard the unmistakable thump when Grampa forgot it was there and walked straight into it. I can still remember Mom telling me after we heard that sound, "Dear, go upstairs and revive your grandpa." And looking around the room, there isn't even a single sign of the fire. There's not even an ax mark in the door where the firemen broke it down. Poor old Grampa.

The attic smells as musty and stuffy as it did when I was five years old. I used to hide up there for hours, just waiting for my sister to sneak up there with another one of the older boys from the neighborhood. And looking out the window, I can still see the tiny little claw marks left on the windowsill by Buck, the cat, as he tried to hold on as my sister pushed him out.

The basement is as damp and dark as I remember it. It was down in the basement that Dad used to play scary games with us like Hang the Pet. In fact, there's still a little piece of rope hanging from one of the beams. As I feel the cool cement on my feet, I remember how careful I used to be. Dad always warned us that it was bad luck to step on an animal's grave.

There'll be a For Sale sign on the old house pretty soon now. Someone will buy it, fix it up, and make it look brand-new. And they'll start building their own treasure chest of memories there. But for me, it will always be my house, the house in which I learned all about life.

Tawn Stein

The Impossible Test

HE WAS SITTING THERE ALL ALONE WHEN I FIRST SAW HIM, A small man hunched over a late-night bar. The place was just about empty. Occasionally his whole body convulsed in a great sob. As I moved closer, I could see he was crying in his beer.

"Mind if I join you?" I said cheerfully, and he indicated the stool next to him. As I sat down, I asked, "Want to talk about it?"

He sighed. "You wouldn't understand," he said softly.

"Try me."

He glanced up at the bartender. "Gimme another one," he said, and then began telling me one of the most incredible stories I'd ever heard.

His name was Kelts, Ben Kelts, and he was a scientist. One day, he explained, he'd accidentally stumbled onto an invention that was going to change medical history and make him rich at the same time. He'd discovered the universal placebo.

96

"You don't understand how important this thing is," he continued. "This was a product that could be made into any form, a pill, solution, anything. It would mimic the characteristics of whatever drug you wanted to test, but with absolutely no side effects. By itself it was completely undetectable. It had no taste, no smell, no effects of any kind at all. You couldn't even tell it was there. It was perfectly safe and cost pennies to make. You know what that means?"

I shook my head.

"Government regulations require that every new drug be tested in a blind study. Half the people get the new drug, the other half get a placebo. My placebo could have been used in every one of those tests. It would have been worth a fortune." As he said those words, his body heaved in a massive sob.

"But that sounds great," I said. "What happened?"

He drained the last of his beer. "The only thing between me and millions of dollars were a few simple government tests."

I didn't understand. "So?"

He laughed bitterly. "So in those tests, what was I going to use as a placebo?"

Michael O'Higgins

"Neuty"

SOMETIMES DREAMS DO COME TRUE. FROM THE TIME LARRY Carty was a little boy, he dreamed of playing football one day for Notre Dame University, the home of his legendary hero, Coach Knute Rockne. But nature was not kind to him. While his heart was big, his body was small, too small even for him to play football in high school. By the time he was fifteen he was barely five feet four inches tall and weighed slightly more than 120 pounds. Still, he refused to give up his dream. "Just watch," he told his friends, "I'm going to play for Notre Dame."

The day the letter arrived from Notre Dame telling him he had been admitted was the proudest day of his life. But for him it was only the beginning. He immediately volunteered to serve the football team as an assistant to the assistant manager, a job consisting of little more than picking up sweaty jerseys and carrying the sports-drink bucket. No one could possibly have done the job any better, though, or with more enthusiasm. From his first day on this job, both the coaches and players liked him.

By the time his sophomore year started, Larry had graduated to assistant manager. His perseverance, his always cheerful attitude, and his dedication to his job made Larry popular. He was always the first to arrive in the locker room for practice; sometimes he even slept there the night before a game. And while Larry loved being with the team, he never gave up his dream of playing for the Irish.

In his senior year Larry Carty was the football team's manager. No one had ever worked harder at the job. By that time the players he had been with for four years knew full well about his dream—and even began lobbying the coaches to put him in for just one play. One play, they implored, more than enough to last a lifetime. But as the season dwindled down, it seemed like an impossible dream.

Notre Dame's final game that season was against Navy. With less than three minutes to play, the Irish led the Midshipmen 63–6. The outcome of the game was no longer in doubt. It was time for Coach Eddie McMahon to spring his surprise. "Carty!" he screamed. "Get a uniform. Quick!"

On the sideline the Notre Dame players joyfully helped him slip into the uniform they'd carefully hidden. There were eighteen seconds left in the game, the regular season, and Larry Carty's career when Coach McMahon said the words Carty had spent his entire life waiting to hear: "Carty. Get in there!"

The entire team huddled around him as Irish quarterback Ray Gilmore called the play. "This one's for you, Larry," he said with a big smile. Then he called

Carty's number. It was the most basic play, a handoff into the line, but it was the biggest moment of Larry Carty's life.

The teams lined up, helmet to helmet. Gilmore called the signals. The ball was hiked. Carty moved forward, legs churning. Gilmore slammed the ball into Carty's stomach and Carty wrapped his arms around it as if he'd been carrying a football forever. He saw daylight between the left tackle and guard and ran for it. He reached the line of scrimmage, protecting the football. As he did, Navy's 280-pound tackle, two linebackers, and a big guard converged on him. They hit him almost simultaneously.

Six surgeons operating for almost eight hours successfully removed the football from Carty's groin. Unfortunately, the rest of the operation was less successful, which is how he earned his nickname, Little Neut.

Steve Judd

An Unspoilt Place

UNEXPECTEDLY, DANIEL DENGATE WALKED OUT OF THE DENSE jungle into paradise. For the famed documentarian, the discovery of West Africa's Golong tribe enabled him to fulfill his lifelong dream. Until Dengate unexpectedly found them living in their Stone Age village in a difficult-to-reach valley, the self-sufficient Golong people had existed only in legend. For what anthropologists estimate is at least one thousand years, the "Lost Tribe" had had absolutely no contact with the outside world. Their primitive life had been totally untouched by modern civilization. This was the last unspoilt place on earth.

Dengate discovered that the Golong people lived in peace and harmony with their magnificent natural surroundings. Their language had no words for enemy or hate or jealousy, they made no weapons, they ate only what they could grow. Man and woman lived together with love based on mutual respect for their lifetime, their children were reverent toward their elders, members of the tribe shared all their possessions and worked happily together. The tribe raised magnificently colored butterflies, which they set free at the full moon as their gift to the gods of nature.

The Golong people had created a paradise on earth, Dengate realized, a living model of how beautiful life could be if people learned to live together peacefully. And he vowed to bring the message of this innocent tribe to the world.

He began by filming the PBS documentary *A Perfect Place*. His twenty-four-person crew lived among the Golong people for six months, learning their customs and their language, while teaching them rudimentary English and introducing them to basic technology, such as Panaflex cameras, cellular phones, and fax machines.

The documentary and accompanying book appealed tremendously to the desire of many people to return to a simpler world. The documentary was nominated for an Academy Award and the book became a big best-seller. Based on this success, Dengate was able to secure financing for the romantic feature film *Love in a Grand Old World*, in which Sandra Bullock starred as a member of a documentary-film crew who falls in love with a widowed Golong man with an adorable young child.

As the Golong "craze" began growing in America, Dengate knew he had to find a way to protect the tribe from exploitation. So he got them the best lawyer in the field, noted theatrical attorney Andrew Glenn.

Glenn immediately negotiated a deal for all rights to manufacture and market authentic Golong woven jewelry, which would be produced in China and sold exclusively on the Home Shopping Network. With proceeds from this sale, the tribe was able to build a small hospital, install a satellite dish, and purchase several big-screen TVs.

Struck by the simple beauty of traditional Golong songs, Barry Manilow recorded an album of authentic Golong music in a recording studio built less than a mile from the village, hiring Golong tribespeople to sing backup vocals.

The opportunity to visit the last unspoilt place on earth proved irresistible to thousands of people, who were willing to spend large sums of money to experience a culture completely free of materialism. To make these tourists comfortable, the Hilton Hotel chain constructed the Golong Resort and Casino, which also provided employment for tribe members.

In addition to the regular tours that began visiting the village, Club Med set up a small village and landing strip within observation distance. Club Med management was able to hire several villagers for full time trainee positions.

Advertisers took note of the public desire to slow down. Chrysler created an entire campaign for a new line of four-wheel-drive vehicles entitled "A New Car for an Old World" around this phenomenon. "Deep in the jungle there is a very special place where life is lived slowly," the narrator said mellifluously, as a brute of a vehicle was seen ripping through the jungle, "but you might not want to spend your whole vacation getting there." The campaign premiered during the Super Bowl. In recognition of their work in this commercial, the Golong people were granted the first tribal membership in Screen Actors Guild history.

When the jungle surrounding the village became overbooked, Disney Inc. was able to convince several members of the tribe to set up a touring unit. This group of Golongs traveled with the "Jack the Ripper on Ice" troupe and lived in small temporary villages in major arenas where ticketholders could observe them. Discounts were given for school groups.

Unfortunately, the worldwide demand for personal appearances by tribespeople made it impossible for them to continue living in their coconut-leaf huts. So, to fulfill commitments made to tour groups, almost one hundred Chinese people were brought into the jungle to lead authentic Golong lives.

Less than four years after he had stepped out of the jungle into ancient history, Dan Dengate's lifelong dream had finally come true: he had earned more money than he ever thought possible and was able to retire to play golf.

Carl Dahl

An Eight-Year-Old
Explains It All

WHEN MY EIGHT-YEAR-OLD SON'S BRITISH COUSIN CAME TO visit him in America for the first time, the two young boys immediately began discussing sports. "I don't understand baseball," nine-year-old London-born Brian Owens said. "It doesn't make any sense to me."

"It's real simple," replied my son, Billy Edgerton. "You have two teams, the owners and the players. The game starts when television stations and the fans give the owners a lot of money. Then the players try to get as much of it as they can from them. At the end of the year, the team with the most money wins."

Brian was impressed. "Sounds like great fun. What else?"

"Well, the game is really run by the officials who call the strikes."

"Oh, I know," said Brian cheerfully, "they're called the umpires."

Billy laughed. "No, silly. They're called union leaders!"

Marilyn Edgerton

The Poet of the Open Road

IN SCHOOL, TEACHERS HELD LITTLE HOPE FOR BILLY MADDEN. He showed no interest in learning. His marks were always poor, he never completed a reading assignment or participated in class discussions, and he rarely did his homework. At an early age he was branded a "nonlearner." Yet, incredible as it might seem, this onetime problem student, who was given up for lost by every one of his teachers, grew up to become one of America's most-read writers!

Leaving high school without a degree, Madden was hired by the State Department of Highways. One day, Madden just happened to be in the office when an emergency occurred. The supervisor charged with writing road signs was out sick, and a sign was desperately needed to warn people not to go too fast. While other people suggested Don't Go Too Fast, and If You Can't Read This Sign You're Going Too Fast, Billy Madden carefully printed the word Slow and a career was born.

Madden had found his niche. He loved writing road signs. Initially, his spelling problems made the job difficult for him. The department unfortunately produced several hundred red, octagonal Stob signs before his misspelling was caught. But Madden spent many sleepless nights overcoming this deficiency and eventually conquered this problem. The result has been tens of thousands of signs that have become familiar to drivers throughout America.

It was Madden, for example, who dauntlessly campaigned to replace the confusing warning Watch Out Deer with the poetic Deer Crossing. For his famed Slippery When Wet, illustrated by wavy tire tracks, he received the first of three coveted Highwayman of the Year awards. Although some of his favorite pieces of writing, such as Big Trains Coming, have yet to make it onto America's highways and byways, the *Guinness Book of World Records* credits Madden as the writer whose words are read most frequently by Americans.

For a young boy once given up on by his teachers as hopeless, America's roads have become his legacy!

Barry Cooper

The Careful Correspondent

In response to criticism that many traditional educational tools are no longer relevant to the lives of today's students, educators have attempted to include in the curriculum materials that students might find useful as they prepare to compete in the twenty-first century. The following example of this is reprinted from "Write Right" with the permission of the publisher:

The importance of communicating distinctly and succinctly cannot be overestimated. Clear, crisp communication is vitally important. The correct choice of words will ensure that the reader understands correctly the point you desire to make. In the following note, identify each of the common errors in communication indicated:

ATTENTION:[1]
I've got your child.[2] **Put a lot of money**[3]

in small bills[4] in a bag[5] and leave it near
a mailbox[6] on Washington and 16th.[7] Do
not contact the police or else.[8]

1. This is a poor salutation. Friendly greetings are
always preferable. Try to address your communication to a specific person or persons if possible.
In this case, "Dear Parents," "Dear Mom," or
even "Friends" would be desirable. And try to
avoid the excessive use of capital letters when not
absolutely necessary.

2. Be specific! Some parents have many children
and this can create confusion as to which child
you have kidnapped. That in turn may cause a
delay in arranging the ransom payment. Whenever possible, identify the person to whom you
are referring by proper name. "I've got your son,
John Jones," would be much better.

3. Before beginning to write a communication of
any type, know exactly what you want to say.
"A lot of money" indicates indecision and can
create a problem for the recipient. Different readers will undoubtedly reach different conclusions
as to how much money is a "lot." Whenever possible, state firmly your needs and desires.

4. When giving instructions, the more specific
you are the less likely the recipient will misunder-
stand. The phrase "small bills" will be interpreted
differently by different people. In this case the
writer might have said "in unmarked twenties."

It is also important to open yourself to new possibilities. Don't get stuck in old patterns. Rather than adhering to kidnapping tradition, for example, the writer might have requested ransom payment be made to an offshore account, or in negotiable bearer bonds, as well as unmarked currency.

5. "A bag" is nonspecific. In any type of business communication try to be assertive. Make the recipient respond to your needs. By demanding the ransom be paid in "a Louis Vuitton overnight bag with a shoulder strap of at least 22" in length," the careful writer demands respect and maintains total control.

6. Sometimes those things you fail to include are more important than what you do include. In this note the writer has failed to specify a time or date for the delivery to be made, making it almost impossible for the recipient to respond. "A mailbox" is much too general, as there may be many mailboxes in this vicinity. When selecting a location for a drop, name a unique place that cannot be misinterpreted.

7. Streets? Avenues? These are common names for locations and can easily lead to a mistake being made in the drop. When giving directions, try to use well-known landmarks. "The mailbox on the southeast corner of Washington Avenue and 16th Street, directly in front of the Wishing Well Tavern" cannot possibly be misinterpreted.

8. Idle threats can lead to disrespect. "Or else" what? Be specific. Give examples of actions that will be taken. Remember, many readers lack imagination. Try to create a picture for the reader with your writing. Don't expect the reader to do your work for you. The careful correspondent gets exactly what he wants, but only if he knows the proper way to demand it.

The Woman Who
Did the Impossible

THEY SAID IT COULDN'T BE DONE. THEY SAID IT WAS IMPOSSI-
ble. That certain accomplishments are simply beyond
human capacity. But that had never stopped people
from trying. A network of Cray superfast computers
created by scientists at Cal Tech had wrestled with the
problem for several weeks but failed to produce the
answer. Most people in the field agreed that this question would continue to tease scientists and mathema-
ticians forever. But none of that stopped Prof. Jordan
Burnett, who refused to accept the impossible.

Working alone on an old Tandy computer, Professor
Burnett solved the problem. And in recognition of this
Herculean effort, Dr. Burnett was awarded the Nobel
Prize in Economics for successfully figuring out which
telephone company offered the lowest rates.

Dr. Burnett's theorem, "No matter what promises
telephone companies make, they will never actually

pay you to use their service," was the basis of the formulas she used to calculate the best possible rates for both local and long-distance calling. The key to solving this problem, Dr. Burnett explained, was to begin by limiting possible solutions to only the most popular three plans offered by the top-rated five hundred telephone companies.

Separating local calls and long-distance calls into distinct categories proved to be a vital component of this formula. The best price for local calls, the professor discovered, can be determined by using the formula:

$$LC = LoC \times TiD/PPM^{(r)} \times SCP/TIC - CC + B/ (T)^N = X$$

meaning local calls (LC) equals the length of the call (LoC) multiplied by the time of day (TiD) divided by the price per minute (PPM) including whether the company rounds to the next minute or charges only for the length of the call (r), multiplied by the specific calling plan used in the calculation (SCP) divided by the type of call (regular or collect) minus the additional expense of using a calling card (CC), plus any offered inducements or bonuses such as frequent-flier miles or cash back (B), with the entire equation multiplied by the number of teenagers with access to the phone $(T)^N$ equals the best possible price for local calls.

Figuring the best value for long-distance calls proved to be slightly more complicated:

$$LD = PC \times LoC \times TiD + Pc^R/PPM \times SCP \times PF/TC - CC + B/ (T)^N = X$$

meaning the best price for a long-distance call (LD) is determined by the place called (PC) multiplied by the length of call (LoC) multiplied by the time of day (TiD) the call is made, plus special phone-company charges (PC) times the rip-off factor (r) divided by the price per minute multiplied by the specific calling plan (SCP), which is multiplied by the amount of money taken out of the system by local or national politicians, divided by the type of call (TC) minus the additional expense of using a calling card plus bonuses such as cash inducements to switch carriers and frequent-flier miles, with the entire equation multiplied by teenagers with access to the telephone $(T)^N$ equals the best possible price.

Reached by reporters on her cellular phone, Dr. Burnett was asked to recommend a specific telephone company. "That's easy," she replied, "Everyone should use the . . ." Unfortunately, before she completed her sentence she left the calling area and could no longer be contacted.

Elizabeth Davis

Step-Mother Teresa

Faith can move mountains, but it's a lot easier with a bulldozer.

—BETTE GLENN

SHE WAS SMALL IN SIZE, BUT HER HEART WAS AS BIG AS THE biggest wallet anyone could imagine. No one knew exactly where she had come from; one day she just seemed to appear on the filthy streets of Calcutta. She wore the habit of a previously unknown religious order. When someone once referred to it as nondenominational, she hastily corrected them, explaining it was "all-denominational." In her hand she tightly clutched a small object that she often held against her chest. It was a simple handheld calculator, but in her hands it was somehow transformed into a powerful machine for change.

She will not be nominated for the Nobel Peace Prize this year, and the media will not sing her praises, but few people have had as much impact on the lives of children as the tiny little woman the people of Calcutta came to know as Step-Mother Teresa.

Unlike her better-known "sister," who felt it was her duty to help other people, Step-Mother Teresa believed it was her duty to teach a simple message: "For yea, I have seen the world around," she quoted Profits 1:04, "and I know thee this: Help yourself. For no matter where people have saken to live, people like to help themselves to everything. Yea."

With all the humor of a fourth-grade teacher in a religious boys school, she brought to Calcutta a discipline no one had ever imagined possible. When most people looked at this city, they saw a place teeming with poor, but friendly people whose families had lived together in harmony for hundreds of years; but she saw something quite different, she saw a smart business opportunity.

The people resisted her strange ways at first, but after she had cracked a few knuckles with the ruler on which she had carefully inscribed the words "Money means nothing without profit," they began to take her seriously. For she had a dream, and she would let nothing stand in her way.

The Calcutta Municipal Orphanage was an old building with drab white walls, a place where children of all ages became old at a young age. They received only a basic education and had no real entrepreneurial spirit. That is, until Step-Mother Teresa arrived with her calculator and brought with her hope that there would a future tomorrow!

Using only her tiny hands to point the way, she ordered these children to do exactly what she wanted. They cleaned the building, painted the walls, and moved furniture. Within weeks the orphanage was transformed into a factory!

At first no one believed in her vision. To other people these were just simple, poorly educated orphans, but to Step-Mother Teresa they were much more than that. To Step-Mother Teresa, these children were what she had been looking for to give meaning to her life—a source of really cheap labor!

Even with a factory and a workforce, it still seemed impossible that work would come to Calcutta. A miracle was needed. But Step-Mother Teresa found courage in her unshakable faith. With all her heart and soul she was devoted to the free-market system. "If you can do it cheaper than they can do it in the Philippines," she promised these simple people, "the contractors will come."

And so they did. A great clothing company, unhappy at being forced to pay workers as much as thirty-four cents an hour, came into the town with its stitching machines. The children sat happily at these machines for many, many hours a day, singing their work songs as they made shirts and blouses.

Yes, Step-Mother Teresa was a stern taskmaster, but she did it with old-fashioned discipline. She often quoted the old American work slogan "If you don't show up Sunday, don't show up Monday." She made sure her workers were paid as much as eighteen cents an hour and took only a small percentage of their wages for food. The factory was so successful that it expanded into rooms once used only a few hours a night by the children as bedrooms, effectively turning once nonproductive space into sewing rooms. But that was only the beginning.

The orphanage is successful now. And the nearby school, the small library, even the rectory, have been turned into clothing factories. The people are making many pennies every day. But none of it could have been possible without the extraordinary commitment of Step-Mother Teresa, the tiny woman who miraculously turned an orphanage in Calcutta into a sweatshop.

David Satin

The Good Agent

RICHARD LANGSAM WAS ONCE THE MOST POWERFUL AGENT IN Hollywood. Representing superstar clients like Clint Eastwood, Barbra Streisand, and James Carrey, he could put a $50-million picture into production or end a career with a single phone call. Langsam's reputation as the ultimate take-no-prisoners negotiator had earned him the nickname Richie Nightmare, a sobriquet of which he was so proud he had it stenciled in gold leaf on his reserved parking spot. He was so powerful, it was said, that owners of restaurants so trendy that no one even knew they existed actually made reservations at his house for dinner. Other agents looked to him with admiration for inspiration and followed his every move. If he took his car to a certain car wash, for example, that car wash immediately became *the* place in town to be seen, and every other agent, producer, director, and actor in Hollywood would soon be found lined up behind him.

But in 1991, Richard Langsam made a left turn into history. Coming out of a shopping center, he turned the wrong way into oncoming traffic. The result was a devastating accident. But his will to survive to deal again was so strong—doctors called it a miracle and the rights to his recovery story were purchased for a TV movie—that within six months he returned to work. But he returned a different man.

Although he proudly wore his scars—causing numerous young agents to visit tattoo parlors for facsimile scars—his brush with death had forced him to look his life squarely in the eye. And he did not like the reflection. And so Richard Langsam decided to change the world.

Within months he had founded The Two Percenters, an organization based on his belief that the top 2 percent of American businessmen could foster significant changes in society by working together to educate this nation's children and to provide assistance to people in need.

To support this program, Richard Langsam announced he would donate 2 percent of all profits earned by his giant talent agency and requested that all other agents in the motion picture and television community follow his example. "It is time," he said, "for those of us who have had the great fortune to be part of this wonderful entertainment industry to give back to the people who have made it possible."

Richard Langsam's unusual request did not go unnoticed. In 1992, in the annual vote by all agents for the prestigious Agent of the Year honors, Richard Langsam finished 14,782nd, directly behind the agent representing Bozo the Clown.

Daniel Hunter

A Most Incredible Life!

HE WAS BORN IN DARKEST AFRICA WHEN RARE SIAMESE-TWIN weak-beaked pigeons collided with the propeller of the single-engine biplane in which his pregnant mother was flying. Incredibly, the propeller perfectly separated the birds, who had been joined at the beak, allowing both of them to survive! The plane crashed, but his mother was thrown 265.5 feet, setting a new world record for airplane-crash survivors, miraculously landing safely in the thick down nest of the Eekie ostrich, a bird that cannot fly but runs as fast as thirty-four miles per hour, when pursued, and is the only known mammal to have no offspring!

She was found there by an albino round nose gorilla, who often grow to be more than eight feet tall and survive on the sap of the beer tree—which yields a liquid remarkably similar in taste and alcoholic content to malt liquor—and carried to the gorilla's den, where her child was born with a large birthmark on his chest in the exact shape of the continent of Africa!

Within a year mother and child were rescued by a party of ten explorers searching for the fabled Lost Tribe of Jungman, who according to legend are born and survive without a sense of humor! In a most amazing coincidence, each member of this rescue party had been born on the twelfth of March, a 2,333,768,343-to-1 chance! On the voyage home, their ship was about to sail into a field of giant icebergs, one of which had been carved by the hand of God as an exact ice portrait of Abraham Lincoln, but they were miraculously saved when a pod of great green whales appeared and nudged the ship to safety, only to disappear never to be seen again!

The ship arrived in New York on the same day that the world's largest venetian blind, consisting of 52,132 slats, was unfurled from the top of the Empire State Building! In New York his mother rented the apartment that had once been the home of Indian fakir Bebe Beebesh, who for the last thirty-five years of his life never spoke a single word that did not begin with the letter *B*, ending on his deathbed with his last words; "Bye bye."

As a seven-year-old boy he learned to play the piano and startled the world of music by composing the Symphony in C-flat, consisting of the note C-flat repeated eighteen thousand times, making it the longest song with only one note ever written!

He was enrolled by his mother in the prestigious Wickshire school, where one of his classmates, Andrew Fox, astonished his friends by simultaneously smoking twenty-four cigarettes before collapsing!

Although he was not born into the Jewish faith, at age thirteen he was bar mitzvahed in a service in which he dumbfounded his relatives by reading a portion of the Torah in ancient Latin, a language in which he had never taken a single lesson, which turned out to be the highlight of this unorthodox bar mitzvah!

Forsaking college, he tried many careers. His first great success was the invention of the game Anti-Monopoly, although he made no money because he gave away all his rights! Eventually, though, he had another idea, and this crazy notion would eventually make him world famous. For this young man's name was Robert Ripley, the creator of *Ripley's Believe It or Not!*

Believe it or not.

Jake Richmond

The Importance of Friendship

WHEN I WAS A LITTLE GIRL, I HAD NO FRIENDS. I HAD NOBODY to play with, nobody to tell all my secrets. But when I was four or five years old, a very special person came into my life. She was my best friend, the friend who was always at my side, through good times and bad; she was my imaginary friend, Irma.

Irma taught me the importance of friendship, and I've never forgotten that. I think real friendship is about the most valuable thing there is, and I would do anything for my friends.

Irma accepted me exactly as I was. She was pretty and smart and nice, and very confident. She was everything I knew I would never be. She wasn't even afraid of adults. We would play together by ourselves for hours and hours. We would play with my dolls and we would dress up in Mom's clothes. We never, ever had a single fight, and we trusted each other with our most important secrets. My mom and dad thought Irma was really cute, and they let her live with me in my room. Mom would even set a place for her at the dinner table.

But sometimes Irma could be very silly. Once, I remember, she went into Daddy's wallet when he was fast asleep and took $30. Then she hid the money under *my* mattress. When Mom found it, she was very mad at me. I told Mom that my invisible friend, Irma, had taken Dad's money, but Mom didn't believe me. She yelled at me a lot. Irma got really mad when Mom said she wasn't real, so she collected all these dead spiders and cockroaches and put them in Mom's shoes. Mom sure was angry when she found them. Irma and I laughed and laughed.

Irma was my best friend in the whole wide world. We went everywhere together. I took her to birthday parties with me even though she was never invited. She went to school with me and during tests she would peek at my neighbor's paper and whisper the answers to me. And she always protected me just like a best friend should. Like there was this boy in my school who was always teasing me? So one day, Irma tripped him and he fell down two flights of stairs.

Irma and I always had so much fun together. When I got older, I started going out with boys. Irma didn't mind, she just wanted me to be happy. And if a boy I liked didn't like me, Irma would go to his house at night and scratch his parents' car. When one boy was really mean to me and called me names, Irma tried to set fire to his house. I don't think anybody ever had such a good friend.

When I went to see Dr. Shaw for my headaches, he told me that Irma was "a little crazy," and that I should make her go away. But I knew that that was not how really close friends treat each other. Real friendship means sticking by someone even when they do something you don't like. And I'll bet anything that Dr. Shaw stopped thinking that after Irma "fixed" the brakes on his car. But I guess no one will ever know what he was thinking all the way down that hill.

When Bobby and I decided to get married, I was afraid Irma would be jealous, but she wasn't, she was really happy for me. I told Bobby about her right away. I thought Bobby might want her to move out, but he didn't; mostly he just pretended she wasn't even there.

Lately, though, Bobby and Irma have become real good friends. In fact, at night sometimes, Bobby gets all dressed up and tells me, "I'm going to take Irma out for a few hours." And then sometimes they stay out all night.

It makes me sad when they leave me home alone, but I don't complain. If I was jealous of Irma, I wouldn't really be a very good friend. Besides, when Bobby goes out with Irma, my new imaginary friend comes to visit. His name is Ted. And he works in the brake repair shop. I think Bobby is going to meet Ted soon.

Allison Lamar

The Danger of
Little White Lies

I WAS WAITING FOR MY WIFE JUST OUTSIDE THE DRESSING room of a big department store when an overweight young woman emerged from one of the stalls wearing a tight dress at least two sizes too small. Posing in front of a mirror, she asked the salesperson, "How does it look?"

"Perfect," the salesperson replied, "it's just right."

I couldn't restrain myself. "Are you kidding?" I said helpfully. "She looks like a three-pound kielbasa stuffed into a hot-dog skin."

The customer burst into tears and retreated to the dressing room. The salesperson eyed me sternly. "Why did you do that? It was just a little white lie. It didn't hurt anybody."

"Oh, but that's where you're wrong," I corrected her, "White lies can be very dangerous." And then I told her the sad story of Andy Smith, the man who told little white lies.

"Just like you," I began, "Andy Smith thought little white lies didn't hurt anybody. One day, for example, he was standing in the street next to a very big dog when a woman asked him, 'Does your dog bite?'

" 'No,' he said. But when she tried to pet this dog, it bit down hard on her hand, drawing blood.

" 'I thought you said your dog didn't bite!' she screamed.

" 'He doesn't,' Andy replied with a big smile, 'but this isn't my dog!'

"Another time Andy was in the theater when the leading man suddenly clutched his heart and fell over. One of the actors came to the front of the stage and pleaded, "Is there a doctor in the house?'

"Andy stood up and shouted, 'Yes!' then moved to the front of the theater. And when he got to the stage and saw the stricken actor, he smiled and said, 'Unfortunately, I'm not him.'

"Finally, one day Andy was flying to California when there was a commotion in the front of the plane. Emerging from the cockpit, a panicked flight attendant shouted, 'Can anybody fly an extremely complicated 757 jumbo jet?'

"Andy couldn't help himself. He had told so many little white lies that it had become second nature to him. He immediately stood up. 'Yes!' he shouted with his usual smile and started making his way to the front of the plane. And when he got there and looked at the complicated controls . . . Well, I'm sure you can imagine what happened after that."

The salesperson looked at me with newfound appreciation. "I see. So what you're saying is—"

"That's right," I interrupted, "in the wrong hands, a little white lie can be fatal!"

"Thank you for sharing that with me, thank you so much. Now I understand why you did that." Then she walked away. But moments later, from somewhere deep inside the dressing room, I heard her voice as she proudly told an unseen customer, "How do you look in that? Are you kidding? You look like an elephant wearing a bikini."

And I smiled contentedly.

Jonathan Wolfe

The Truth About Them

THROUGHOUT HISTORY, BRAVE MEN AND WOMEN OF SCIence have been willing to risk scorn and ridicule to defend unpopular beliefs. For almost twenty-five years Prof. Lawrence Kimball worked alone on a secret project in a dingy basement laboratory at the Institute of Human Studies. When he was not there, his lab was locked and no one, not even maintenance, was permitted entry. He never discussed his project with his colleagues, hinting only that he was on the verge of a discovery that might someday earn him recognition in the annals of science.

Finally, at the annual symposium, he asked to be recognized. Striding to the podium, his glasses falling down his nose, his wild hair flowing in a slight breeze, he cleared his throat and said, "I am pleased to be able to report the results of the study of my lifetime. Ladies and gentlemen, I have found irrefutable evidence that there is a direct relationship between breast size and intelligence!"

The room erupted. Angry voices shouted at him. The director of the institute stood up and said, "I can tell you, Professor Kimball, that that is about the dumbest thing I have ever heard."

Professor Kimball did not back down in the face of ridicule. As men of science have done for hundreds of years, he defended his research. "Not only that," he shouted above the din, "my research shows that results are the same whether the subject has breast implants or natural breasts!"

"This is absurd," the director said, "this is ridiculous."

"You're wrong," the professor insisted, holding up his thick report. "I have proof. It is right here. There can no longer be any doubt, the larger the breasts, the dumber the man."

Overcoming the Last Taboo

MIKE GORDON WAS DRIVING HIS LATE-MODEL SEDAN ALmost seventy miles an hour on the freeway when, without warning, it happened. Suddenly he became aware of a strange feeling in his throat. It began to grow bigger and bigger. He gasped for air. But it was not enough. The feeling continued to grow. The seconds ticked by like hours. He tried to focus on the road. He tried to ignore the feeling, but it was impossible. He opened his mouth as wide as he could, fighting for every last drop of air, desperately trying to quell that feeling. He forced fresh oxygen down his throat. And then . . . just as suddenly as it had begun, it was over. Until the next time.

This is the terrifying story of a yawn. It happened to Mike Gordon—and it could happen to you! Mike Gordon was lucky—this time. Although compelled to yawn, he was able to maintain control of his car until the yawn passed. But many other people have not been so fortunate.

At one time or another every one of us has suffered the terrible embarrassment of yawning. Perhaps you had just met an extremely desirable person or were just listening to the boss outlining marketing strategy when it happened. You suddenly felt that desperate need for air, that not-so-funny tickle at the base of your throat. You tried desperately to fight it, you swallowed hard, you tried to drag in air with your mouth closed, but nothing worked. Nothing. Eventually, you yawned. You opened your mouth as wide as possible and breathed in deeply, feeling the cool flow of oxygen satisfying this primal urge. And it felt so good, so pleasurable. You didn't mean to do it. You didn't want to do it. But you couldn't help it. You yawned. Right in the face of a loved one or your employer or supervisor or teacher or friend. Instantly, an entire relationship was changed forever. All because of a simple yawn that could have been prevented.

Yawning is one of this country's least discussed afflictions. To some people a yawn may seem to be little more than a nuisance, a pressure on your throat that can easily be satisfied, but a yawn at the wrong time can prove disastrous. A jumbo jet pilot, for example, had just begun his final approach to landing at the world's busiest airport. He was focusing on dozens of cockpit instruments while getting instructions from the tower. The fate of three hundred people depended on his actions in the next few seconds. Suddenly he felt that unmistakable tickle in his throat. It took an act of incredible will for him not to yawn, and the plane landed safely.

A young man from Austin, Texas, sadly recalled the moment that changed his life. Just as he was about to propose to the woman he loved, he began yawning. His proposal was ruined, and they never married.

An actor auditioning for Steven Spielberg lost his chance for a featured role in *Jurassic Park* when he could not stifle a long, pleasurable yawn.

Most people are too ashamed or embarrassed to confess that they suffer from Chronic Yawning Syndrome, or CYS. Yawning may well be the last taboo. But it doesn't have to be that way. Not anymore. Nobody has to yawn! No longer do you have to be held hostage to the fear of yawning.

Until now, it has been accepted that yawning is a natural phenomenon that cannot be prevented. But research conducted by Dr. Franklyn Biondo of the National Center for Yawning Control has proven that that is not necessarily true. Dr. Biondo believes that anyone can be taught to overcome yawning within six to eight weeks.

Dr. Biondo's training program, which is currently available through his infomercial "How to Not Yawn!" recommends several different techniques that will successfully combat that deep-rooted urge to lift your arms way up into the sky, stretch your arms out as far as you can, open your mouth, and suck air! Among these methods are behavior modification, in which the potential yawn is nipped before it can be triggered; beta-wave control, in which new thoughts are substituted in an effort to trick the mind; and hard candy, which acts to soothe the feathered-throat mechanism.

"The fact is, you can stop unsightly and potentially dangerous yawning right now," Dr. Biondo says flatly. "We all recognize how really good and satisfying a great big yawn feels, but there is a proper time and place for it. Gaining control of your yawn is the beginning of gaining control of your whole life."

No one is immune to yawning. It happened to Mike Gordon. It can happen to you! It is time to take action to overcome . . . the last taboo.

Herb Cohn

The Incredible Power Within

NONE OF US REALLY KNOWS HOW WE WILL REACT IN A crisis—until we are faced with a situation in which every single second counts. Some people panic. But many others find within themselves an inner strength that they never knew existed. History is replete with stories of ordinary people who performed extraordinary physical feats or found brilliant solutions when faced with life-threatening problems.

For Valerie Shore of Reynoldsville, Mississippi, that crisis came on a hot Tuesday afternoon in 1992. It had been a routine day. She had spent it as she did most days, washing clothes, cleaning the trailer, cooking, and doing whatever chores her husband, Jethro, ordered. After sixteen years of marriage, she had long since surrendered any hope of change in her life.

It was just after two o'clock when she heard a terrible scream. She immediately recognized Jethro's angry yelling, but it was different this time; this time it was not directed at her. She ran out of the trailer and instantly realized what had happened. Jethro had been working beneath an old car, trying to repair the brakes. Somehow, it had slipped off the cinder blocks and trapped him. His arm and one leg were being held down in the soft mud by the wheel. "Damn it, Valerie," he screamed at her, "I'm caught. Don't just stand there like an idiot. Get some help."

Valerie looked at the car. She guessed it weighed more than a ton, more than any one person could ever move without help. "Can you move at all?" she asked.

"What's the matter with you? What does this look like? I'm trapped."

She looked around for help. There was no one else as far as she could see. She was his only hope. "You sure you can't move?" she shouted.

He snarled at her in pain. "If you don't call for some help right now, when I get outta here, you're gonna be real sorry."

The car shifted, pushing his arm down even farther into the mud. He screamed loudly in pain. Valerie knew she had little time to act. She knew if she didn't take action right then and there, it would be too late. And at that moment, Valerie Shore found the strength she had never known existed. From where it came she would never know. Acting calmly, she raced back into the house. In seconds she'd found their bankbook and all her husband's cash. Within minutes, she had packed up a few belongings and was speeding toward the bank, desperately trying to get there before it closed.

For on that day, when faced with a crisis, Valerie Shore saved her own life. By the time the rescuers she had alerted got to their trailer to help Jethro, she had cleaned out their account, and Jethro never heard from her again.

How I Found
the Secret of Happiness

I HAD SPENT MUCH OF MY LIFE SEARCHING FOR THE TRUE SE-cret of happiness. I crossed deserts, I climbed mountains, and I sat at the feet of gurus. But still I felt this great emptiness inside. Then one day I saw the author Deepak Chopra on television and he looked so happy I immediately read his best-selling books *The Seven Spiritual Laws of Success* and *The Way of the Wizard.*

Still, though, something was missing, something I couldn't explain. Then I saw Leo Buscaglia on a talk show and was incredibly impressed with the joy he projected, so I read his best-selling books *Personhood; Living, Loving and Learning;* and *The Way of the Bull.*

Although they were fascinating, they didn't seem to have the answer I needed. So I attended a seminar given by Wayne Dyer. He seemed so content, so centered, that he appeared to me to have found what I so badly wanted. So I bought his best-selling books

DAVID FISHER

Your Erroneous Zones and *Staying on the Path* and read them twice from cover to cover.

These books contained valuable advice and important suggestions, but none of this information made me feel happy deep inside. Robert Fulghum appeared on a talk show and I liked his no-nonsense approach to finding happiness in life, so I read his best-selling books *All I Really Need to Know I Learned in Kindergarten* and *It Was on Fire When I Lay Down on It*. For almost a full day after completing these books I could feel something stirring inside me. Could it be? I wondered. But a day later that feeling was gone, so I suspect it had been caused by bad food.

If anybody had truly discovered the secret of happiness, I realized, it had to be M. Scott Peck, whose *The Road Less Traveled* has been a best-seller for a decade and given joy to millions of people. On his best-selling inspirational video, Peck seemed to be completely at peace with himself, just the way I wanted to be. So I read all his books, including *Further Along the Road Less Traveled* and *The Different Drum*. They made such good sense, but somehow they didn't provide the solution to my quest. I just knew it was out there somewhere, so I kept searching for it.

So many people told me they had learned so much from Marianne Williamson that I went to hear her lecture, then read her best-selling book *Return to Love*. Her thoughts seemed to make such good sense, but still left me wanting more, wanting to find what she had so obviously found.

I was plagued by worry and self-doubt. I knew there was a secret, all of these people seemed to have found it. What could it be? I wondered. What could

142

these people have found that continued to elude me? And finally, like a bolt out of the blue, it came to me. One day, I discovered the secret of happiness. It had been right in front of me the whole time. To find happiness, I realized so clearly, just as all of these fine writers had done, all I had to do was make a small fortune writing my own best-selling inspirational book.

About the Author

DAVID FISHER has dedicated his life to eliminating hypocrisy at a profit. He is a man of intrigue and mystery. He is the author of the prize-winning novella *Conversations with My Cat, Hard Evidence: Inside the FBI's Sci-Crime Lab,* as well as the best-sellers *Gracie* with George Burns, *The Umpire Strikes Back* with Ron Luciano, and the reference book *What's What*. He lives in New York City with his fantasies.